THE MEANING OF HITLER

The Meaning of Hitler

SEBASTIAN HAFFNER

TRANSLATED BY
EWALD OSERS

MACMILLAN PUBLISHING CO., INC.

NEW YORK

Originally published in Germany under the title
Anmerkungen zu Hitler, copyright © 1978 by
Kindler Verlag GmbH München

Macmillan Publishing Co., Inc.
866 Third Avenue, New York, N.Y. 10022

Library of Congress Catalog Card Number: 79-89431
ISBN 0-02-547290-9

First American Edition 1979

Printed in the United States of America

Contents

Life   1

Achievements   23

Successes   47

Misconceptions   73

Mistakes   97

Crimes   123

Betrayal   147

Life

ADOLF HITLER's father made a success of life. The illegitimate son of a servant girl, he rose to become a state official of administrative rank and died honoured and respected.

His son began by making a mess of his life. He did not finish school, failed his entrance examination at the Vienna Academy of Arts, and spent the time from his eighteenth to his twenty-fifth year in Vienna and then in Munich, doing nothing and aspiring to nothing. His orphan's pension and the occasional lucky sale of a painting kept the young Bohemian afloat. At the outbreak of war in 1914 he volunteered for the Bavarian Army. There followed four years of front-line service, during which courage earned him both classes of the Iron Cross but lack of leadership qualities prevented him from rising above the rank of corporal. After the end of the war, which he witnessed as a gas casualty in a German military hospital, he remained a 'barracks dweller' for a further year. He still had no plans or prospects of a job. He was then thirty.

At that age, in the autumn of 1919, he joined a small radical Right-wing party, in which he soon played a leading role, and that was the beginning of a political career which eventually made him an historic figure.

Hitler lived from 20 April 1889 until 30 April 1945, i.e. almost exactly fifty-six years. The difference between his first thirty and the following twenty-six years seems to be inexplicable. For thirty years he was an obscure failure; then almost overnight a local celebrity and eventually the man around whom the whole of world policy revolved. How does that go together?

Although that difference has provoked numerous explanations it is in fact more apparent than real, not merely because Hitler's political career continued to be disjointed during its first ten years, and Hitler the politician turned out in the final analysis to be a failure, albeit on a supreme scale, but mainly because Hitler's personal life remained poor and stunted even during the second, public, period of his life. By contrast, closer inspection of his inner political life during the first, outwardly uneventful, decades of his

3

life reveals many unusual features – features which foreshadowed much that followed.

The division which certainly marks Hitler's life does not cut across it but runs through the whole. Not all weakness and failure before 1919, all vigour and achievement after 1920. But before and after an exceptional intensity of political living and feeling alongside an exceptional meagreness of personal experience. The obscure Bohemian of the pre-war years was living and inwardly working on the political scene of his day as though he were a top politician; and the Führer and Reich Chancellor remained, in his personal life, a successful Bohemian. The decisive characteristic of his life is its one-dimensionality.

Many biographies carry as a sub-title under their hero's name: 'His life and times', with the word 'and' dividing rather than uniting. Biographical and historical chapters alternate; the great individual stands, in the round, before a background of two-dimensional contemporary events. He stands out from his time as much as he intervenes in it. A life of Hitler cannot be written in that way. Everything that matters in it blends with history, *is* history. The young Hitler reflected it; the man of middle years still reflected it but began to influence it; the later Hitler determined it. First he was made by history, then he made history. That is worth looking at. The personal side of Hitler's life consists essentially of non-events – after 1919 as much as before. Let us dispose of them briefly.

His life lacked – 'before' *and* 'after' – everything that normally lends weight, warmth and dignity to a human life: education, occupation, love and friendship, marriage, parenthood. Apart from politics and political passion, his was an empty life and hence one which, though certainly not happy, was strangely lightweight, and lightly discarded. A continuous readiness for suicide accompanied Hitler throughout his political career. And at its end, almost as a matter of course, stood a real suicide.

Hitler's celibacy and childlessness* are well known. Love

---

* It has lately been claimed that, as a soldier in France in 1917, Hitler fathered an illegitimate son on a French woman. Even if this is correct, Hitler never knew him. The experience of fatherhood is lacking in Hitler's life.

played an unusually slight part in his life. There were a few women, but he treated them as unimportant and did not make them happy. Eva Braun attempted suicide twice because she felt hurt and neglected ('He only needs me for certain purposes'); her predecessor, Hitler's niece Geli Raubal, actually did commit suicide – probably for the same reasons. Hitler was on an election tour and had not taken her along; her action compelled him, for once – the only time – to interrupt something that was more important to him, for her sake. Hitler mourned her and replaced her. This melancholy story is what comes closest to a great love in Hitler's life.

Hitler had no friends. He enjoyed sitting for hours on end with subordinate staff – drivers, bodyguards, secretaries – but he alone did all the talking. In this 'servants' quarters atmosphere' he unwound. Real friendship he avoided all his life. His relationships with men such as Goering, Goebbels or Himmler always remained cool and remote. Röhm, the only one of his paladins with whom he was on familiar terms from early days, he had shot, principally, no doubt, because he had become politically inconvenient. However, the old intimacy certainly proved no obstacle to his removal. If one reflects on Hitler's general shyness one is almost led to suspect that Röhm's superannuated claim to friendship was, if anything, an additional reason for getting rid of him.

There remain education and occupation. Hitler never enjoyed any systematic education; just a few years of *Realschule* (a lesser type of school), with poor reports. True, during his years of loafing he read a lot but – on his own admission – absorbed only what he thought he already knew. In the political sphere Hitler had the knowledge of a dedicated reader of newspapers. His only real learning was of military affairs and military technology. Here the practical experience of the front-line soldier enabled him critically to absorb what he read. Strange though it may sound, his front-line experience was probably his only education. For the rest, he remained the typical half-educated man all his life – one who always knew better and tossed about picked-up pieces of half-knowledge and wrong knowledge, preferably before an audience whom he could impress by doing so because it knew nothing at all. His table talk at his headquarters testifies to his educational gaps in an embarrassing manner.

Hitler never had nor sought an occupation; on the contrary, he positively avoided one. His shyness of occupation is as striking a trait as his shyness of marriage or intimacy. Nor could one call him a professional politician. Politics was his life but never his profession. During his early political career he variously gave his occupation as painter, writer, merchant and propaganda speaker; later he was quite simply the Führer, not answerable to anyone – at first only the Führer of the Party but ultimately *Der Führer* altogether. The first political office he ever held was that of Reich Chancellor; viewed from a professional point of view he was a strange chancellor: he left the capital whenever he chose, read or did not read documents as and when he pleased, held Cabinet meetings only irregularly and after 1938 not at all. His political mode of working was never that of the top public servant but that of an unfettered independent artist waiting for inspiration, seemingly idle for days and weeks on end, and then, when the spirit moved him, throwing himself into a sudden frenzy of activity. Only in the last four years of his life did Hitler, for the first time, practise a regular activity – as military Commander-in-Chief. Then, of course, he could not play truant from the twice-daily staff conferences. And then his inspiration increasingly failed him.

It might be objected that poverty or non-existence of a private life is not unusual in men who dedicate themselves totally to a great goal of their own choosing and who have the ambition to make history. That is not so. There are four men with whom Hitler, in each case for a different reason, calls for comparison, though he does not stand up to it – Napoleon, Bismarck, Lenin and Mao. None of these, not even Napoleon, failed so frightfully as Hitler, which is the main reason why Hitler does not stand comparison with them. But we shall leave this aside for the moment. What we want to point out in the present context is that none of them was a nothing-but-politician like Hitler and a nonentity in all other fields. All four were highly educated and had a profession in which they had proved themselves before

6

'going into politics' and going down in history: general, diplomat, lawyer, teacher. All four were married; Lenin was the only one without children. All knew great love – Josephine Beauharnais, Katarina Orlov, Inessa Armand, Chiang Ch'ing. That makes those great men human, and without their complete humanity something would be lacking in their greatness. Hitler lacks that something.

He lacks something else that needs mentioning briefly before we come to what is really worth considering in Hitler's life. There is no development, no maturing in Hitler's character and personality. His character was fixed at an early age – perhaps a better word would be arrested – and remains astonishingly consistent; nothing was added to it. It was not an attractive character. All soft, lovable, reconciling traits are missing unless one regards his shyness, which sometimes seems like bashfulness, as a reconciling feature. His positive characteristics – resolution, boldness, courage, perseverance – lie all on the 'hard' side. The negative ones even more so: ruthlessness, vindictiveness, faithlessness and cruelty. Added to these, moreover, from the very start, was a total lack of capacity for self-criticism. Hitler was all his life exceedingly full of himself and from his earliest to his last days tended to self-conceit. Stalin and Mao used the cult of their personality coolly as a political instrument, without letting it turn their heads. With the Hitler cult, Hitler was not only its object but also the earliest, most persistent and most passionate devotee.

Enough said about the person and the unprofitable personal biography of Hitler. Let us now look at what is worth looking at, his political biography which, in contrast to his personal one, is not short of development or intensification. It begins long before his first public appearance and reveals seven stages or leaps:

1. His early concentration on politics as a substitute for life.
2. His first (still private) political action – the emigration from Austria to Germany.
3. His decision to become a politician.
4. His discovery of his hypnotic abilities as a mass-audience orator.

5. His decision to become *Der Führer*.

6. His decision to adapt his political timetable to his personal expectation of life (this is simultaneously his decision to wage war).

7. His decision to commit suicide.

The last two decisions differ from the preceding ones in that they are solitary decisions. With all the others the subjective and objective sides are inseparable. They may be Hitler's decisions, but in Hitler or through Hitler the spirit of the age or the mood of the day each time acts like a gust of wind filling a sail.

Even the emerging passionate political interest of the eighteen- or nineteen-year-old, who had suffered the shipwreck of his artistic ambition but carried ambition as such into his new sphere of interest, was in tune with or indeed sprang from the mood of the day. Europe before the first war was far more political than today. It was a Europe of great imperialist powers – all in permanent rivalry, all jockeying for position, all in permanent readiness for war. That was exciting to everybody. It also was a Europe of class conflicts and of the promised or feared Red Revolution. That too was exciting. In one way or another, politics was the subject at any table of regulars at a middle-class café and in any proletarian tavern. The private lives, not only of the workers but also of the middle classes, were much narrower and poorer than they are today. But in the evening, as a compensation, everyone was, with his country, a Lion or an Eagle, or, with his class, the banner-bearer of a great future. Hitler, who had nothing else to do, was that all day long. Politics was then a substitute for living – for almost everyone to a certain extent, but for the young Hitler wholly and exclusively.

Nationalism and socialism were powerful mass-mobilizing slogans. Imagine the explosive power if one succeeded in somehow uniting them! It is possible, though not certain, that this idea occurred even to the young Hitler. He wrote subsequently that even at the age of twenty, in Vienna about 1910, he had laid 'the granite foundations' of his political ideology – but whether that ideology is justified in calling itself National Socialism is open to argument. The real Hitlerian bedrock, his primal and lowest

8

layer, which took shape during his Vienna period, is certainly not a fusion of nationalism and socialism but a fusion of nationalism and anti-semitism. Anti-semitism was the primary element, and this Hitler carried with him from the start, like a congenital hump. But his nationalism too, a very special Greater-German nationalism, undoubtedly dates back to his time in Vienna. His socialism, however, is most probably a later addition.

Hitler's anti-semitism is an East European plant. In Western Europe and also in Germany anti-semitism was on the wane about the turn of the century; assimilation and integration of the Jews was desired and was in full swing. But in Eastern and South Eastern Europe, where the numerous Jews were living, voluntarily or involuntarily, as a separate nation within the nation, anti-semitism was (and is?) endemic and murderous, directed not towards assimilation or integration but towards liquidation and extermination. And this murderous East European anti-semitism, which allowed the Jews no escape, reached as far as Vienna in whose third district, according to Metternich's famous dictum, the Balkans begin. There the youthful Hitler picked it up. How, we do not know. There is no record of any disagreeable personal experience, and he himself never claimed anything of the kind. According to his account in *Mein Kampf* the observation that Jews were different people was enough for the conclusion, 'Because they are different they have to be removed.' The way in which Hitler later rationalized that conclusion will have to be discussed in a later chapter, and the way he put it into effect in a later chapter still. For the moment that murderous anti-semitism of the East European variety, which penetrated deeply and firmly into the young man, remained without practical consequences even in his own obscure life.

Not so his Greater-German nationalism, the other product of his Vienna years. In 1913 it gave rise to the first political decision of his life – his decision to emigrate to Germany.

Young Hitler was an Austrian who did not feel himself to be an Austrian but a German and, what is more, a disadvantaged German, one left in the lurch, one unjustly excluded from the

Reich at its foundation. In feeling that way he was sharing the sentiments of many German Austrians of his day. With the whole of Germany behind them, Austria's Germans had been able to rule over their multi-national empire for centuries and to impress their stamp on it. Since 1866 they had been excluded from Germany, and thus they had become a minority in their own empire, helpless in the long run against its many nationalities, condemned to practising a hegemony (one then shared with the Hungarians) for which their strength and number were no longer sufficient. From such a precarious situation a great variety of outcomes were possible. The young Hitler, always a great one for drawing conclusions, drew the most radical one. Austria was bound to break up, but in that break-up a Greater German Reich must emerge that would again embrace all German Austrians and which would then, by its weight, again dominate the small countries which were its co-heirs. In spirit he no longer regarded himself as an Austrian Royal and Imperial subject but as a citizen of that Greater German Reich to come. And from this he drew certain conclusions for himself, again the most radical ones: in the spring of 1913 he emigrated.

We know now that Hitler emigrated from Vienna to Munich in order to avoid service in the Austrian Army. That this was not due to draft dodging or cowardice is proved by the fact that, when war broke out in 1914, he immediately volunteered for active service, but in the German and not the Austrian Army. By 1913 war was in the air, and Hitler did not wish to fight for a cause from which he had inwardly dissociated himself, nor for a state which he regarded as doomed. He was still a long way from wishing to become a politician – how indeed could he have become one in the German Empire as a foreigner with no occupation? But he was already acting politically.

During the war Hitler was politically happy. Only his anti-semitism remained unsatisfied. If he had had his way the war would have been used to exterminate 'internationalism', which he misspelt and by which he meant the Jews, within the German Empire. But otherwise things all went splendidly for four years –

victories and more victories. Defeats were suffered only by the Austrians. 'With Austria things will go the way I always said,' he wrote in his know-all manner from the front to acquaintances in Munich.

We now come to Hitler's decision to become a politician – one of many he has described as 'the hardest of my life'. Objectively this was made possible by the revolution of 1918. In Imperial Germany a foreigner of Hitler's social position could not have even begun to develop any political activity, except possibly in the Social Democratic Party, which did not suit Hitler and which, moreover, as far as influence upon real state policy was concerned, was a blind alley. The revolution, however, opened the path to power in the state for the existing political parties and simultaneously so thoroughly upset the traditional party system that even new parties now stood a chance. In 1918 and 1919 numerous new parties were founded. Apart from all this, Hitler's Austrian citizenship was now no longer an obstacle to active participation in German politics. True, the incorporation of 'Deutschösterreich' – the German residual part of the Austrian monarchy – had been forbidden by the victorious powers; however it was passionately desired on both sides of the frontier and it was psychologically anticipated – so much so that an Austrian was virtually no longer regarded as a foreigner in Germany. And after a revolution which had abolished the rule of princes and the privileges of the nobility there were now no social barriers for any German politician.

We emphasize this point because it is always overlooked. Hitler, as is well known, introduced himself into politics as the sworn enemy of the 1918 revolution, the 'November Crime', and therefore we are reluctant to see him as its product. But objectively he *was* its product, just as Napoleon had been a product of the French Revolution which he too, in a certain sense, overcame. Both men would be inconceivable without the revolutions which preceded them. Neither restored what the revolution had abolished. They were its enemies but they accepted its legacy.

November 1918 – and in this case we may believe Hitler – provided the impetus for his decision to go into politics, even though he did not actually take this decision until the autumn of 1919. However, November 1918 was the experience that aroused him. 'There must never again be and there will never again be a November 1918 in Germany', was his first political *resolution* after a great many political ponderings and speculations. It was the first specific objective the young private politician set himself and incidentally the only one he truly accomplished. There was certainly no November 1918 in the Second World War – neither a timely termination of a lost war nor a revolution. Hitler prevented both.

Let us be clear about what this 'never again a November 1918' implied. It implied quite a lot. First of all the determination to make impossible any future revolution in a situation analogous to November 1918. Secondly – since otherwise the first point would be left in the air – the determination to bring about once more a similar situation. And this implied, thirdly, the resumption of the war that was lost or believed to be lost. Fourthly, the war had to be resumed on the basis of a domestic constitution in which there were no potentially revolutionary forces. From here it was not far to the fifth point, the abolition of all Left-wing parties, and indeed why not, while one was about it, of all parties. Since, however, one could not abolish the people behind the Left-wing parties, the workers, they would have to be politically won over to nationalism, and this implied, sixth, that one had to offer them socialism, or at least a kind of socialism, in fact National Socialism. Seventh, their former faith, Marxism, had to be uprooted and that meant – eighth – the physical annihilation of the Marxist politicians and intellectuals who, fortunately, included quite a lot of Jews so that – ninth, and Hitler's oldest wish – one could also, at the same time, exterminate all the Jews.

It will be seen that Hitler's domestic policy programme was almost complete at the moment he entered politics. Between November 1918 and October 1919, when he became a politician, he had of course had sufficient time to clarify and sort everything out in his mind. And one has to concede that he was not lacking in the talent to clarify an idea to himself and draw conclusions. He had not lacked it even during his early years in Vienna, any more than he had lacked the courage to implement radically in practice the conclusions he had theoretically, and again radically, drawn. It is, of course, worth noting that the entire edifice of his ideas was based on a fallacy – the fallacy that the 1918 revolution had been the cause of defeat. In fact it had been its consequence. But then that was a fallacy which Hitler shared with a great many Germans.

His triggering experience of 1918 did not yet provide him with a foreign policy programme. He only developed that during the following six or seven years, but we will briefly deal with it now. Initially there was only the decision at all costs to resume the war which, in Hitler's opinion, had been prematurely discontinued. Then came the idea of planning the new war not simply as a replay of the old one but under new, more favourable constellations, exploiting the conflicts which had torn asunder the enemy coalition during and after the First World War. We shall omit the phases through which the development of this idea ran and the various possibilities with which Hitler toyed during the years 1920 to 1925; they can be found in other books. The final result, at any rate, as laid down in *Mein Kampf*, was a plan which envisaged Britain and Italy as allies or benevolent neutrals, the Austro-Hungarian successor states and also Poland as auxiliary nations, France as a secondary enemy to be eliminated at the start, and Russia as the principal enemy to be conquered and permanently subjected, and to be turned into German living space, 'a German India'. That was the plan underlying the Second World War, though it went wrong right from the start when Britain and Poland did not accept the roles intended for them. We shall come back to this point later, as we are now dealing with Hitler's political development.

We are now at the point of Hitler's entry into politics and public life, in the autumn and winter of 1919/20. This was his breakthrough experience following the awakening experience of November 1918. The breakthrough was not so much the fact that he rapidly became the leading figure in the German Workers' Party (which he presently renamed the National Socialist German Workers' Party). That did not require a lot. The party, when

Hitler joined it, was an obscure back-room organization with a few hundred members of little importance. The breakthrough experience was his own discovery of his power as an orator, which took place on 24 February 1920, when, with sweeping success, he made his first speech at a mass rally.

Hitler's ability to transform rallies of the most varied individuals – the bigger and the more motley the better – into a homogeneous pliable mass, to put that mass first into a kind of trance and then to give it something like a collective orgasm, is well known. It was based not so much on his skill as a speaker – Hitler's speeches got going slowly and hesitantly, they had little logical structure and at times barely a clear content; moreover, they were delivered in a hoarse, rough, guttural voice – as on a *hypnotic* ability, the ability of a concentrated willpower to gain control of a collective subconscious wherever it made itself available and at any time. That ability of mass hypnotism was Hitler's first, and for a long time his only, political capital. As to its power, there are countless testimonies from those affected by it.

More important still than the effect on the masses, however, was the effect on Hitler himself. This can only be understood if one tries to imagine a man who had reason to regard himself as impotent suddenly finding himself capable of performing miracles of potency. Even in the past, among his army comrades, Hitler had occasionally switched from his normal reticence to sudden furious talk and heated argument if the conversation turned to what moved him most profoundly – politics and the Jews. Then he had only produced mild astonishment and earned himself the reputation of a 'crank'. Now the 'crank' suddenly discovered himself as one who could move the masses, as the 'drummer', the 'king of Munich'. The quiet bitter pride of the despised man thus turned into the intoxicated self-assurance of the successful.

He now knew that he could do something no one else could. He also knew, at least in domestic politics, exactly what he wanted; and he could not fail to notice that none of the other far more prominent politicians of the Right-wing scene, where he now became a figure, really knew what they wanted. The two discoveries together were bound to give him a sense of uniqueness to which he had always, even as a failure and an 'unrecognized genius', and perhaps especially then, inclined. From this gradually arose what was probably the greatest and most revolutionary decision in his political life – the decision to become *Der Führer*.

That decision cannot be dated, nor was it triggered off by one particular event. We may be certain that it was not present during the initial years of Hitler's political career. Hitler then was content to have become the propaganda speaker, the 'drummer', of a national revivalist movement. He still stood in awe of the fallen leaders of Imperial Germany who used to gather in Munich at that time and hatch plans for the most diverse *coups d'état*; especially of General Ludendorff who had directed the German war effort during its last two years and was now the recognized central figure of all revolutionary Right-wing movements.

Upon closer acquaintance Hitler lost that awe. The consciousness of his assured domination of the masses, which he shared with no one, came gradually to be accompanied by a sense of political and intellectual superiority over all conceivable rivals. At some point or other there must have also come the further realization – a realization by no means a matter of course – that this rivalry was not just about the share-out of posts or the order of precedence in a future Right-wing government but about something in fact unprecedented – the position of an all-powerful permanent dictator, uninhibited by any constitution or division of powers, without any strings of collective leadership.

Here the vacuum was revealed which the disappearance of the monarchy had left behind and which the Weimar Republic was unable to fill since it was accepted neither by the revolutionaries of November 1918 nor by their opponents. It remained, as a well-known slogan put it, a 'republic without republicans'. There emerged in the Germany of the early twenties a mood in which, in Jacob Burckhardt's words, 'the yearning for something analogous to the former powers became irresistible' and which 'was working towards the *one man*'. It was not only as a substitute for their lost Kaiser that a large part of the nation was longing for 'the *one man*', but also because of bitterness over the lost war and impotent anger against what was felt to be an insulting dictated peace treaty. The poet Stefan George voiced a widespread mood when, in 1921, he prophesied an age which

Brings forth the one who helps, the Man

and at the same time mapped out his tasks for him:

He bursts the chains, restores on fields of rubble
His order, scourges those who've gone astray
Back to eternal justice, where the great
Is great again, and master once more master,
Obedience reigns, and on the people's banner
Pins the true sign and through wild storm and terror
Of the red dawn he leads his faithful band
To the day's deed – the New Reich's planting.

Almost tailor-made for Hitler! Even the 'true sign', the swastika, had (admittedly without anti-semitic overtones) been adorning Stefan George's books for several decades. Indeed an earlier verse of George, dating back to 1907, also seems like an early vision of Hitler:

The man! The deed! Thus pine both people and High Council.
Do not expect one who dined at your tables!
Perhaps one who for years sat among your murderers,
*Slept in your cells, will rise and do the deed.**

---

* Stefan George (1868–1933), an important poet (though scarcely read today) and founder of a Men's League, emerges in many parts of his later writings, since 1907, as the prophet of the Third Reich. It is significant that he did not like the Third Reich at all when it eventually arrived. He escaped the great official tributes planned for his sixty-fifth birthday on 12 July 1933, by emigrating to Switzerland, where he died the same year. One of the members of the George circle and one of the last disciples of the ageing poet was Count Claus Stauffenberg who performed the attempt on Hitler's life on 20 July 1944 and paid for it with his life. Originally he had enthusiastically hailed Hitler's seizure of power. The chapter of German intellectual history entitled 'George – Hitler – Stauffenberg' still remains to be written.

It is unlikely that Hitler knew George's verses but he knew the widespread mood they expressed, and this acted upon him. Nevertheless the decision to be himself 'the Man' for whom all were waiting and of whom all were expecting miracles undoubtedly required a certain wild courage which no one other than Hitler had then or later. In the first volume of *Mein Kampf*, dictated in 1924, this decision is presented as fully matured, and when the Party was re-established in 1925 it was for the first time put into effect formally. In the new NSDPA there was, from the outset and once and for all, only *one* will – that of the Führer. The fact that his decision to be the Führer was subsequently realized on a far greater scale is, as far as Hitler's internal political development was concerned, a lesser leap than his original decision to venture it at all.

The intervening period, according to how one calculates it, amounted to six, nine or even ten years, since, even in 1933, Hitler did not attain the complete omnipotence of the 'Führer' who is answerable to no one. This only happened after Hindenburg's death in 1934. Hitler was forty-five when he became *Der Führer*. This now raised the question for him of how much of his domestic and foreign policy programme he would be able to achieve within his lifetime; and he answered that question with the most extraordinary political decision of all, one that is still not universally known, and the first one he kept entirely secret. His answer was: the lot! And this answer implied a monstrosity, the subordination of his politics and of his political timetable to the presumable duration of his earthly life.

It was, in the most literal sense, an unprecedented decision. After all, the life of man is short, that of states and nations is long. All constitutions, republican as well as monarchist, are based upon that fundamental fact as a matter of course. Even the 'great men' who want to 'make history' make allowance for it, either by reason or by instinct. Thus, none of the four men with whom we have compared Hitler postulated or practised his irreplaceability. Bismarck built himself a powerful but clearly defined post in a constitutional system planned to endure, and when he had to vacate that post he did so, angrily but obediently. Napoleon tried to found a dynasty. Lenin and Mao organized the parties which they had founded also as nurseries for their successors, and these parties have indeed produced capable successors and – though often amidst crisis and bloodshed – eliminated incapable ones.

None of this applies to Hitler. He deliberately based everything upon his own irreplaceability, upon an eternal 'I or chaos'. One might almost say upon 'After me the Deluge'. There was no constitution, no dynasty – which, of course, would have been anachronistic, quite apart from Hitler's aversion to marriage and his childlessness – , but equally no truly state-supporting, solidly constructed party organization capable of surviving and repro- ducing leaders. To Hitler his party was merely the instrument of his own seizure of power. It never had a Politburo and he never allowed a crown prince to emerge. He refused to think beyond, or to make provision beyond, his own life-span. Everything had to happen through himself.

With that decision, however, he placed himself under a time pressure that was bound to lead to precipitate and inappropriate political decisions. Any policy, in fact, is of necessity inappropriate if it is governed not by the circumstances and possibilities of a given situation but by the probable duration of an individual life. But that was just what Hitler's decision implied. More particularly it implied that his planned great war for 'living space' would have to be waged in his own lifetime and by himself. Naturally he never discussed that publicly. No doubt the Germans would have been a little alarmed if he had done so. But in the notes he dictated to Bormann in February 1945 he openly admitted it all. Having complained that he had started the war one year too late, in 1939 instead of in 1938 ('But I could not do anything since the British and French accepted all my demands at Munich'), he continued: 'I must now disastrously accomplish everything within the short span of a human life ... where others had an eternity at their disposal, I only have a few miserable years. The others know that they will have succeessors ...' But then he had himself seen to it that he would not have one.

At the outbreak of the war in 1939 he also allowed it to be understood a few times, though never publicly, that he was determined to align and subordinate the history of Germany to his personal biography. When the Romanian Foreign Minister Gafencu visited Berlin in the spring of 1939 he said to him: 'I am now fifty; I would rather have the war now than when I am fifty-five or sixty.' To his generals, on 22 August, he justified his 'unalterable decision in favour of war' by referring among other things to the 'rank of his personality and its incomparable authority' which might perhaps not be available at a later date: 'No one knows how long I have to live.' And a few months later, on 23 November, speaking to the same group and urging them to speed up their plans for the Western offensive: 'As a final factor I must, in all modesty, list my own person: irreplaceable. Neither a military nor a civilian personality could take my place. Attempts on my life may be repeated ... the fate of the Reich depends on me alone. I shall act accordingly.'

Ultimately, therefore, this was a decision to subordinate history to autobiography, the destinies of states and nations to his own life – an idea of truly breathtaking perversion and overweening pride. Just when it took possession of Hitler cannot be established. In its germ it is, of course, present in Hitler's concept of the Führer, a concept that had crystallized by the mid twenties. From the absolute non-answerability of the Führer to his absolute irreplaceability is not a great step. Nevertheless there are some indications that Hitler did not take this step, which after all was also the decisive step towards war, until the latter part of the thirties. The first recorded indication is the secret conversation of 5 November 1937, contained in the so-called Hossbach Minutes, when he revealed to his most senior ministers and military men the first and as yet rather vague glimpse of his war plans and by doing so gave them a nasty fright. It probably required the astonishing successes of his first years of government, successes not expected even by himself, to magnify his self-assurance to the point of superstition, to a sense of being specifically chosen, a sense which not only justified him in equating himself with

Germany but ('the fate of the Reich depends on me alone') aligning and subordinating Germany's life and death to his own life and death. That, at any rate, was what in the end he did.

Yet for himself life and death had always been close to each other. His end, as is well known, was by suicide, but that suicide did not come out of the blue. He had always, in the event of failures, inclined in that direction and he had spelt it out that he was prepared at any time to throw away the life upon which he had made Germany's fate depend. After the failure of the Munich *putsch* of 1923 he said to Ernst Hanfstaengl, at whose home he was initially hiding, that he would now make an end of it and shoot himself, and it took Hanfstaengl, by his own account, some effort to talk him out of it. In a later crisis, in December 1932, when the Party was threatened by a split, he remarked to Goebbels, who has testified to it: 'If the Party falls apart I'll make an end of it in five minutes with my pistol.'

In view of his real suicide on 30 April 1945 these cannot be dismissed as mere words. In the remarks to Goebbels the three words 'in five minutes' are particularly revealing. In subsequent remarks, always on the same pattern, they became seconds, and finally even 'the fraction of a second'. Hitler clearly concerned himself all his life with the thought of how swiftly suicide could be accomplished and how easy it therefore was. After Stalingrad he voiced his disappointment at Field-Marshal Paulus's failure to shoot himself instead of surrendering to the Russians with the following explosion: 'The man should shoot himself, just as the ancient generals used to throw themselves upon their swords when they saw that things were lost ... How can anyone be afraid of that second in which he can free himself from misery, unless duty holds him back in this vale of tears! Well!' And after the attempt on his life on 20 July 1944: 'If my life had come to an end then for me personally – I can say this – it would have merely been a liberation from worries, sleepless nights and grave nervous disease. It is only the fraction of a second, and then one is freed from all that and has one's quiet and eternal peace.'

In consequence, when it really happened, Hitler's suicide

scarcely caused surprise. It was registered almost as a matter of course, and by no means because suicide by those responsible is generally a matter of course after lost wars. It is anything but that, in fact it is exceedingly rare. It seemed a matter of course because Hitler's life seemed in retrospect to have been designed towards that end from the start. Hitler's personal life had been too empty to seem to him to be worth preserving even in disaster; and his political life was, almost from the start, a life of all or nothing. When nothing came up suicide followed as if automatically. As for the specific courage required for suicide Hitler always had it, and if one had asked oneself one would always have credited him with it. In the end, strangely enough, he was scarcely blamed for committing suicide; it seemed all too natural.

What did seem unnatural and almost embarrassingly out of style was the fact that he took his mistress, who had meant little to him in life, with him to his death, and, with a strangely touching petit-bourgeois effect-spoiling gesture, had secretly married her during the twenty-four hours preceding their joint end. What, fortunately for him, did not become known until much later – because that would have been *greatly* resented, and rightly so – was the fact that he had also tried to take Germany, or what was left of it, with him to his death. That point, and Hitler's relationship with Germany generally, will be discussed in the final chapter under the heading 'Betrayal'.

In the meantime we shall take a closer look now at Hitler's extraordinary achievements and his, to his contemporaries at the time, even more astonishing successes. Because, beyond any dispute, these existed.

Achievements

D URING the first six years of his twelve-year reign Hitler astonished friends and enemies alike with a series of achievements which hardly anyone would have thought him capable of. It is these achievements which at the time confused and inwardly disarmed his opponents – in 1933 still a majority of Germans – and which to this day give him a certain secret prestige among sections of the older generation.

Previously Hitler had only enjoyed the reputation of a demagogue. His performances as a mass audience speaker and a mass hypnotist had, of course, always been undisputed and during the years of the Depression, which reached their peak in 1930–32, had, from one year to the next, made him an increasingly serious candidate for power. But scarcely anyone expected that, once in power, he would prove successful. Running the country, everybody was saying, was after all rather different from making speeches. It was also noticed that in his speeches – in which he immoderately berated the government, demanded all power for himself and his party and, unconcerned about contradicting himself, flattered the malcontents of all hues – he never made a single specific proposal. For instance he said nothing about what should be done to halt the Depression and unemployment, the overriding worry at the time. The author Kurt Tucholsky voiced the opinion of many when he wrote: 'The man does not really exist – he is only the noise he makes.' When, after 1933, the man turned out to be an exceedingly energetic, inventive and efficient operator, the psychological reaction was great.

Admittedly, one thing, additional to his powers as an orator, would have been noticed by observers and judges of Hitler even prior to 1933 if only they had looked at him a little more closely – his organizing talent or, more accurately, his ability to create for himself efficient power machines and to dominate them. The NSDAP of the late twenties was wholly and entirely Hitler's creation; as an organization it was already superior to any other party even before, in the early thirties, it began to rally the mass vote

25

behind it. It far outstripped the famous old party organization of the Social Democratic Party of Germany; even more than that party during the Imperial period, the NSDAP was already a state within the state, an alternative state on a small scale. And in contrast to the Social Democratic Party, which had soon become ponderous and self-sufficient, Hitler's NSDAP possessed an uncanny dynamism from the start. It obeyed only *one* dominating will (Hitler's ability to tame or eliminate almost effortlessly rivals and opponents within the party was also a trait which attentive observers should have noticed as early as the twenties), and it was, down to the smallest units, full of fighting spirit, a hissing and pounding steam-engine of an electoral machine, of a kind previously unknown in Germany. Similarly, Hitler's second creation of the twenties, his civil war army, the SA, made all other political fighting units of the day – the Nationalist *Stahlhelm*, the Social-Democratic *Reichsbanner*, and even the Communist *Roter Frontkämpferbund* – appear like lame Philistine clubs by comparison. It far outstripped them all in fighting spirit and aggressiveness, and, of course, also in murderous brutality. Among the political private armies of the day the SA alone was genuinely feared.

It was, incidentally, this fear, deliberately fanned by Hitler, that ensured that the terrorism and violations of law which accompanied Hitler's seizure of power in March 1933 aroused so little outrage and opposition. Worse had been expected. For a whole year the SA, with bloodthirsty anticipatory joy, had heralded a 'night of long knives'. This did not take place; there were only sporadic, secret and rapidly suppressed – though never punished – murders of a few particularly hated opponents. Hitler had personally and solemnly (under oath, as a witness in the Reich Court) announced that after his assumption of power heads would roll, the heads of the 'November criminals'. After that it almost came as a relief when the veterans of the 1918 revolution and the prominent figures of the Republic were 'merely' locked away in concentration camps during the spring and summer of 1933. They were subjected to brutal maltreatment and existed in danger of their lives, but sooner or later most of them got out again. A few even remained entirely undisturbed. The public had expected pogroms; instead there was only a one-day – 1 April 1933 – boycott of Jewish shops, and it passed off bloodlessly and remained essentially symbolical. In short, everything was very bad but nevertheless a little less bad than anticipated. Those who, rightly as it would turn out, were saying 'All this is only the beginning' were apparently proved wrong when, during 1933 and 1934, the terror slowly died down to give way, during 1935–37, to the 'good' Nazi years, to almost normal conditions only slightly disturbed by the continued existence of the now less crowded concentration camps. For the moment those who had said 'All these are only regrettable excesses of transition' seemed to have been right.

On the whole, the management and dosage of terror during the first years must be described as a masterly psychological achievement by Hitler. First came creation of fear by wild threats, then severe terror measures but nevertheless falling somewhat short of the threats, and finally gradual transition to a near-normalcy, but without complete renunciation of a little background terror. It ensured, among those who initially rejected him, or who wanted to wait and see – i.e. the majority – , the right measure of intimidation without driving them into desperate opposition; and, more importantly, without diverting their attention too much from the more positive accomplishments of the regime.

Among these positive achievements of Hitler the one outshining all others was his economic miracle. The term did not then exist; it was coined, much later, for the astonishingly rapid reconstruction feat of the Erhard era in Western Germany after the Second World War, but it applies even better to what was taking place in Germany under Hitler during the mid thirties. There was then a much deeper and stronger impression that a real miracle was being accomplished, and that the man who accomplished it, Hitler, was a miracle worker.

In January 1933, when Hitler became Reich Chancellor, there were six million unemployed in Germany. A mere three years later, in 1936, there was full employment. Crying need and mass hardship had generally turned into modest but comfortable prosperity. Almost equally important: helplessness and hopelessness had given way to confidence and self-assurance. Even more miraculous was the fact that the transition from depression to economic boom had been accomplished without inflation, at totally stable wages and prices. Not even Ludwig Erhard succeeded in doing that later in post-war Western Germany.

It is difficult to picture adequately the grateful amazement with which the Germans reacted to that miracle, which, more particularly, made vast numbers of German workers switch from the Social Democrats and the Communists to Hitler after 1933. This grateful amazement entirely dominated the mood of the German masses during the 1936 to 1938 period and made anyone who still rejected Hitler seem a querulous fault-finder. 'The man may have his faults, but he has given us work and bread again' was the million-fold view during those years of former Social Democrat and Communist voters who in 1933 had still represented the great mass of Hitler's opponents.

Was the German economic miracle of the thirties really Hitler's achievement? In spite of all conceivable objections one will probably have to reply in the affirmative. It is entirely true that in matters of economics and economic policy Hitler was a layman; in the main the various ideas with which the economic miracle was set in motion did not come from him. In particular that giddy piece of financial virtuosity on which everything depended was clearly the work of another man, his 'financial wizard' Hjalmar Schacht. But it was Hitler who had appointed Schacht and who had given him a free hand, first to run the Reichsbank and then also the Ministry of Economic Affairs. And it was Hitler who had fished out from their pigeonholes all those reflation plans which had existed before him but which, before him, had fallen victim to all kinds of reservations, mainly of a financial nature. Hitler had them put into effect, from special tax vouchers, to the Labour Service, and to the autobahn. He was not a political economist and he had never dreamed that he would rise to power by way of

28

an economic slump and with the task of liquidating mass unemployment. That was not his kind of task at all; economic matters, prior to 1933, had played virtually no part in his plans or political thinking. But he possessed enough political instinct to grasp that they were playing the main part just then and, surprisingly, he also had enough economic instinct to understand – unlike, for instance the unfortunate Chancellor Brüning, one of his predecessors – that expansion was more important at that moment than budgetary or monetary stability.

In addition, of course, unlike his predecessors, he also possessed the power to impose, by force, at least the *semblance* of monetary stability. After all, we must not disregard the seamy side of Hitler's economic miracle. Since it was taking place amidst a continuing world-wide depression and was making Germany an island of prosperity, it required the isolation of the German economy from the outside world; and since its financing, of its very nature, was inevitably inflationary it required the imposition from above of fixed wages and prices. For a dictatorial regime, with concentration camps in the background, both these things were possible. Hitler had no need to consider either the employers' associations or the trade unions because he could forcibly bring the two together in the 'German Labour Front' and thus paralyse them. And it was just as easy for him to lock up in a concentration camp any entrepreneur conducting unauthorized foreign business or raising the prices of his goods as it was to lock up any worker demanding higher wages, let alone threatening to strike for them. To that extent, too, the economic miracle of the thirties must be described as Hitler's accomplishment, and to that extent there was even a certain logic on the side of those who, for the sake of the economic miracle, were prepared to accept the concentration camps.

The economic miracle was Hitler's most popular achievement but not his only one. At least as sensational, and just as unexpected, was the re-militarization and rearmament of Germany which was likewise successfully accomplished during the first six years of his rule. When Hitler became Reich Chancellor Germany had an army of 100,000 men without modern weapons, and it had no air force. By 1938 it was the strongest military and air power in Europe. An incredible achievement! This, too, would not have been possible without certain preparatory work during the Weimar period, and again it was not Hitler's own work down to the last detail but in the main a tremendous achievement of the military establishment. But it was Hitler who gave the order and provided the inspiration. The military miracle is even less conceivable without Hitler's decisive impetus than the economic miracle, and even more than the economic miracle, which was an improvisation on Hitler's part, it stemmed from his long-cherished plans and intentions. That it did not, in Hitler's hands, subsequently work to Germany's benefit is a different matter. It remains an achievement nevertheless, and, just as the economic miracle, an achievement of which no one beforehand would have thought Hitler capable. That he accomplished it against all expectations produced amazement and admiration, though perhaps also a certain measure of anxiety on the part of some people. (What did he want all that frenzied rearmament for?) However, most people reacted to it with satisfaction and national pride. In the military as in the economic sphere Hitler had proved himself a miracle worker and only the most obdurate know-alls could now deny him their gratitude and allegiance.

Two aspects of Hitler's rearmament policy need only brief mention, but a third one calls for more detailed comment.

First, it has often been claimed that Hitler's economic miracle and his military miracle were basically the same thing, that full employment was entirely, or at least predominantly, due to rearmament. That is not so. Certainly conscription removed a few hundreds of thousands of potential unemployed from the streets, and the mass production of tanks, guns and aircraft provided wages and livelihood for a few hundreds of thousands of metal and engineering workers. But the great bulk of the six million unemployed whom Hitler had inherited found re-employment in entirely normal civilian industries. Goering, who uttered a lot of boastful nonsense in the course of his life, then coined the misleading slogan of 'guns instead of butter'. In actual fact, the Third Reich was producing guns *and* butter, and a great many other things.

Second, rearmament also had an important foreign policy aspect. It meant the invalidation of vital sections of the Versailles Peace Treaty, and hence a political triumph over France and Britain, and a radical transformation of the balance of power in Europe. This will be discussed in a different context in the chapter headed 'Successes'. At this point, when we are dealing with Hitler's achievements, it is the achievement as such that concerns us.

Third, this achievement, however, contains in itself a very personal contribution of Hitler's, one which deserves a moment's closer consideration. We have mentioned that the enormous detailed work of rearmament had not been Hitler's job but that of the War Ministry and the General Staff. This statement needs qualification. On one particular point of detail, one that was later to prove of great importance in the war, Hitler personally intervened and laid down the structure of the new Wehrmacht and hence its future manner of operation. He took the decision, against what was then still the overwhelming majority of the military experts, to create integrated, independently operating armoured divisions and tank armies. These novel army formations, possessed in 1938 only by the German Army, proved to be the campaign-deciding weapon during the first two years of the war. They were subsequently copied by all other armies.

Their creation was Hitler's personal work and represents his greatest accomplishment in the military field, an accomplishment greater than his controversial generalship during the war. Without Hitler the minority among the generals – represented chiefly by Guderian – who had recognized the potential of an independent armoured force would probably not have prevailed in Germany against the conservative majority, any more than it did in Britain or France, where the advocates of armour, Fuller and de Gaulle, were baulked by the opposition of the traditionalists. It is probably no exaggeration to say that the campaigns of 1939 to 1941,

31

especially the campaign in France in 1940, were decided before they even took place, in these internal military controversies which scarcely aroused any interest among the public. The fact is that Hitler then took the right decision, although it made him decidedly unpopular among the conservative military men at the time. But it paid off later, in his military triumph over France in 1940, a triumph which momentarily confused even the last and most steadfast of his German opponents.

But even earlier, in 1938, Hitler had succeeded in winning over to himself the great majority of those who in 1933 had still voted against him – perhaps his greatest achievement of all. It was an achievement which the surviving older generation finds embarrassing and the posthumous younger generation incomprehensible. Today the 'How could we?' of the old and the 'How could you?' of the young trip easily off the tongue. At the time, however, it required a quite exceptional perception and farsightedness to recognize in Hitler's achievements and successes the hidden seeds of future disaster, and it required quite exceptional strength of character to resist the effect of those achievements and successes. His speeches, with their barking and foaming at the mouth, which nowadays cause revulsion or laughter when listened to again, were delivered at the time against a background of facts which deprived the listener of the strength to contradict even internally. It was that background of facts which produced the effect, not the barking and foaming at the mouth. Here is an excerpt from Hitler's speech of 28 April 1939:

I overcame chaos in Germany, restored order, enormously raised production in all fields of our national economy ... I succeeded in completely resettling in useful production those seven million unemployed who so touched all our hearts ... I have not only politically united the German nation but also rearmed it militarily, and I have further tried to liquidate that Treaty sheet by sheet whose 448 Articles contain the vilest rape that nations and human beings have ever been expected to submit to. I have restored to the Reich the provinces grabbed from us in 1919; I have led millions of deeply unhappy Germans, who had been snatched away from us, back into the Fatherland; I have restored the thousand-year-old historical unity of German living space; and I have ... attempted to accomplish all that without shedding blood and without inflicting the sufferings of war on my people or any other. I have accomplished all this ... as one who 21 years ago was still an unknown worker and soldier of my people, by my own efforts ...

Sickening self-adulation. A ridiculous style ('those seven million unemployed who so touched all our hearts'). But, damn it, it was all true, or nearly all. Anyone clutching at those few points which were perhaps not quite true ('Overcame chaos' – without a constitution? 'Restored order' – with concentration camps?) was bound at times to feel just a petty nit-picking know-all. As for the rest, how could anyone challenge that in April 1939? After all, the economy really was flourishing. The unemployed had again been given work (there had not been seven million but six – but who was counting?); rearmament was a fact; the Treaty of Versailles had really become a scrap of paper (and who, in 1933, would have thought that possible?); the Saarland and the Memel territory really belonged to the Reich again, as did the Austrians and Sudeten Germans, and they were really happy about it – their jubilations still rang in peoples' ears. Miraculously it had actually been brought about without war, and no one could dispute that twenty years earlier Hitler really had been an unknown person (not exactly a worker, but never mind). Had he created everything by his own efforts? Of course, he had had helpers and collaborators, but could one seriously maintain that everything would have turned out the same without him? Could one therefore still reject Hitler without rejecting all that he had accomplished, and, set against these achievements, were not his unpleasant traits and misdeeds merely blemishes?

What the old opponents of Hitler, the educated and cultured middle class, and even believing Christians or Marxists, were

33

bound to ask themselves in the mid thirties and late thirties in the face of Hitler's undeniable achievements and his never-ending miracles was: Can it be that my own yardsticks are wrong? Can it be that not everything I was taught or that I believed in is right? Am I not being proved wrong by what is happening here before my own eyes? If the world – the economic world, the political world, or the moral world – were really such as I had always thought it to be then surely such a man would have suffered shipwreck in the quickest and most ridiculous way. Indeed he could never have got as far as he had got! But in fewer than twenty years he has turned from being a complete nonentity into the central world figure, and everything comes out right for him, even the seemingly impossible, everything, everything! Does this not prove something? Does it not compel me to revise all my concepts, including aesthetic and moral concepts? Should I not, at least, admit that I was mistaken in my expectations and predictions, and should I not be very restrained now in my criticism and very careful about my judgement?

Such self-doubts are entirely understandable and indeed attractive. But from there to the first still half-reluctant 'Heil Hitler' was but a small step.

Those converted or semi-converted by the spectacle of Hitler's achievements did not as a rule become National Socialists, but they became followers of Hitler, believers in the Führer. And they, at the peak of the general faith in the Führer, were certainly more than 90 per cent of all Germans.

A colossal achievement to have united virtually the entire nation behind him – and accomplished in less than ten years! Accomplished, moreover, on the whole not by demagogy but by achievement. When, in the twenties, Hitler had at his disposal nothing but his demagogy, his hypnotic oratory, his intoxicating and illusionist skills as a producer of mass spectacles he hardly ever gained more than 5 per cent of all Germans as his followers; in the Reichstag elections of 1928 it was 2.5 per cent. The next 40 per cent were driven into his arms by the economic plight of 1930–33 and by the total helpless failure of all other governments and parties in the face of that plight. The remaining, decisive, 50 per cent, however, he gained after 1933 mainly through his achievements. Anyone who, say in 1938, uttered a critical remark about Hitler, in circles where that was still possible, would inevitably, sooner or later – sometimes after half-hearted agreement ('I don't like that business with the Jews either'), – have received the answer, 'But look at all the things the man has achieved!' Not, for instance, 'But isn't he an enthralling speaker!'; nor, 'But wasn't he wonderful again at the last Party Rally!'; and not even, 'But look at his successes!' No, it was, 'But look at all the things the man has achieved!' And what, in 1938, or still in the spring of 1939, could one really reply to that?

There was yet another phrase that was in continual use by Hitler's newly won followers at that time. It was, 'If the Führer only knew!' It suggested that faith in the Führer and conversion to National Socialism were still two different things. The things people did not like about National Socialism – and there were still many people who disliked a great deal – they tried, instinctively, to separate from Hitler. Objectively speaking, that was of course incorrect. Hitler was just as responsible for the destructive measures of his regime as for the constructive ones. In a certain sense the destruction of the constitutional state and the constitutional texture – points we shall return to later – must also be called 'achievements' of Hitler, achievements of destruction loaded with as much power as his positive achievements in the economic and military spheres. Somewhere between these lie his achievements in the social sphere. In them the destructive and constructive elements are balanced.

During the twelve years of his rule Hitler carried out great social changes. However, these must be carefully differentiated.

Three major social transformation processes began in the late phase of Imperial Germany, continued during the Weimar Republic and also under Hitler, and are still continuing all the time in the Federal Republic and in the German Democratic Republic. They are, first, the democratization and equalization of society, or in other words the end of the privilege of birth and the lowering

35

of class barriers; second, the revolution of sexual morality, or in other words the progressive depreciation and rejection of Christian asceticism and bourgeois decency; third, the emancipation of women, that is the progressive levelling of sex discrimination in the legal system and the world of employment. In these three areas Hitler's achievement, whether positive or negative, was relatively slight, and we are mentioning it here only because there is a widespread mistaken idea that he halted or reversed those three trends.

This emerges most clearly in the emancipation of women which, as is well known, was, on paper, rejected by National Socialism. In actual fact, it made great leaps forward, especially during the second six-year span of the regime, during the war, and then with the full approbation and often vigorous support of party and state. Never before had women moved into so many male occupations and male functions as during the Second World War, and this process was no longer reversible – and probably would not have been reversible even if Hitler had survived the Second World War.

In the area of sexual morality the National Socialist attitude was, on paper, inconsistent. There was much praise for 'German chastity and morality', but there was also loud contempt for 'sermonizing hypocrisy and Philistine stuffiness', and there was no objection to 'healthy sensuality' especially if, within or outside wedlock, it ensured a supply of healthy young Germans. In practice the trend towards the cult of the body and of sex, which had started in the twenties, continued unchecked in the thirties and forties.

As for the progressive abolition of class privilege and the removal of class barriers, they were entirely in line with official National Socialist policy. In contrast, the Italian Fascists pinned to their banners the restoration of a 'corporate state', i.e. a stratified state, which is one of several reasons why Hitler's National Socialism and Mussolini's Fascism should not be jumbled up together. The National Socialists only changed the socialist vocabulary; what used to be called the 'classless society' was called by them the 'national community'. But in practice it was the same thing. It is undeniable that under Hitler, even more so than during the Weimar period before him, there was a great deal of vertical movement upwards and downwards, an inter-mingling of classes and a break-up of class barriers, that was a 'green light to the man with ambition', especially if he was a Party sympathizer. By no means everything was a pretty sight, but it was undeniably 'progressive', in the sense of progress towards greater equality. This trend was personally encouraged by Hitler in the Officer Corps, which, in the 100,000-man army allowed to the Weimar Republic, had been the almost exclusive preserve of the aristocracy. Hitler's first field-marshals, those who came from the Weimar Reichswehr, nearly all still had a 'von' in front of their names; hardly any of the later ones had.

All this is by the way and mentioned only for completeness's sake. As we have said, these were developments which had begun before Hitler and continued under and after him, developments which Hitler's activity affected but slightly, either negatively or positively. But there was *one* great social transformation that was Hitler's personal work and that, interestingly enough, has been reversed in the Federal Republic while it has been preserved and further developed in the GDR. Hitler himself called it the 'socializa-tion of people'. 'Why should we need all that – socialization of banks and factories,' he had said to Rauschning. 'What does it matter once I have the people firmly fitted into a discipline from which they cannot escape ... we are socializing the people.' It is the socialist side of Hitler's National Socialism that we must now examine.

Anyone who, along with Marx, sees the essential or even the sole characteristic of socialism in the public ownership of the means of production will naturally deny that socialist side of National Socialism. As Hitler did not nationalize any means of production he was no socialist – this settles the matter for the Marxists. But careful! It is not as simple as all that. Surely it is an interesting point that none of the present socialist states con-fined themselves to the socialization of the means of production.

37

They expended a great deal of effort on also 'socializing the people', in other words organizing them collectively, as far as possible, from the cradle to the grave, pressing them into a collective 'socialist' way of life, 'firmly fitted into a discipline'. It is a valid question whether this, in spite of Marx, is not the more important aspect of socialism.

One is used to thinking in terms of the conflicting categories of socialism and capitalism. But it would probably be more correct, and certainly more important, to see not capitalism but individualism as the opposite of socialism. After all, in the industrial age, socialism is also quite inevitably a kind of capitalism. Even a socialist state must accumulate, renew and expand capital. The way a manager or engineer works or thinks is exactly the same under capitalism and socialism; and factory work, even in a socialist state, is inevitably alienating work. Whether the machine or the conveyor belt he services belongs to a private firm or to a nationalized enterprise makes no discernible practical difference to the worker at his job. What does make a great difference, however, is whether, once he has finished work, he is left to do what he chooses or whether a 'collective' – one might also say a community – is waiting for 'him at the factory gate. In other words, more important than a person's alienation from his work – about which nothing very much can probably be done in an industrialized economy under any system – is his alienation from his fellow beings. Or to put it another way, if the goal of socialism is the liquidation of human alienation then the socialization of people will attain that goal far more effectively than the socialization of the means of production. The latter course may eliminate an injustice, even though, if the past thirty or sixty years are anything to go by, at the cost of efficiency. The former really does liquidate an alienation, viz. the alienation of big-city humans from one another, even if at the cost of individual freedom. Freedom and alienation are just as much two sides of the same coin as community and discipline.

Let us put this in specific terms. Where the lives of the vast majority of Germans, who were not racially or politically rejected or persecuted, differed in the Third Reich from their life in pre-Hitler Germany, and also from that in the present Federal Republic, and where they resembled present life in the GDR like two peas in a pod, was that by far the greatest portion of them took part in extra-domestic communities or 'collectives' which the majority, whether membership was officially compulsory or not, were unable in practice to avoid. Schoolchildren belonged to the *Jungvolk* just as in the GDR today they belong to the Young Pioneers; the adolescent found a second home in the Hitler Youth just as he does today in the Free German Youth; men of active age practised military sports in the SA or SS just as they do today in the Society for Sport and Technology; women were active in the German Women's League just as now, in the GDR, they are in the Democratic Women's League; and anyone who was anyone or wanted to be anyone belonged to the Party, in the Third Reich as much as in today's GDR. Not to mention the hundreds of National Socialist (or now socialist) occupational, hobby, sports, educational or leisure activity associations. Strength Through Joy! Beauty of Labour! Of course, the songs that were sung and the speeches that were made were different in the Third Reich from those in the GDR today. But the activities, rambling, marching and camping, singing and celebrating, model-making, PT and firearms drill, were indistinguishable, just as much as the undeniable sense of security, comradeship and happiness which flourish in such communities. In that he forced the people into that happiness Hitler undoubtedly was a socialist – indeed a very effective socialist.

Was it happiness? Or did the compulsion make people feel unhappy? In the GDR at present people often try to escape from their enforced happiness; but when they get to the Federal Republic they just as often complain about their loneliness, which is the other side of the coin of individual liberty. Things were probably similar in the Third Reich. We shall not try here to decide the question of who is happier, socialized man or man living as an individual.

Altogether the reader will have noticed (possibly with disap-

pointment) that in this chapter, which deals with Hitler's achievements, we have been very sparing with value judgements. That
lies in the nature of the matter. Achievements as such are morally
neutral. They can only be positive or negative, not good or evil.
Hitler did a lot that was evil, and we shall have more than enough
opportunity in later chapters to condemn him morally. But one
should not condemn him for the wrong reasons – a mistake that
had to be paid for heavily at the time and one that is still often
being made. 'Never belittle the devil!' There has always been a
great temptation to underestimate Hitler because of the shabby
and ridiculous sides of his personality; that temptation is even
greater now that he has failed. One should try to resist it.

Of course one hesitates, and justly so, to call him a 'great man'.
'Those who are only vigorous destroyers are not great at all' says
Jacob Burckhardt, and Hitler certainly proved himself a vigorous
wrecker. But beyond any doubt he also proved himself a star
achiever of high calibre, and not only in wrecking. Admittedly,
without his decidedly exceptional vigour the disaster which he
accomplished would have turned out less enormous, but one
should not lose sight of the fact that his road to the abyss led
across high peaks.

In the prologue to his biography of Hitler, Joachim Fest
performs an interesting speculative experiment. He says:

If Hitler had succumbed to an assassination or an accident at
the end of 1938, few would hesitate to call him one of the
greatest of German statesmen, the consummator of Germany's
history. The aggressive speeches and *Mein Kampf*, the anti-
semitism and the design for world dominion, would presumably
have fallen into oblivion, dismissed as the man's youthful
fantasies . . . Six and one-half years separated Hitler from such
renown.

'Six years', as Fest writes at another point in his book, 'of gro-
tesque errors, mistakes upon mistakes, crimes, convulsions, destructive mania and death.'

Quite certainly Fest does not mean that Hitler's errors, mistakes and crimes only belonged to his last six years; indeed Fest superbly reveals in his book how deep their roots go back to Hitler's early years. However, Fest is entirely right in saying that they only came to full effect or fruition during the second half of his rule, while during the first half they were masked by unexpected achievements and successes which Hitler himself had intended only as preparatory actions. Fest is also right in presenting the autumn and winter of 1938/39 as the apogee of Hitler's career: until that date things were going upwards, but from then onwards decline and fall were preparing themselves – or were prepared by him. Certainly most Germans, if he had then died as a result of an attempt on his life (or indeed of an accident or a heart attack), would have felt that they had lost in him one of their great men. But would they have been right, and would one still think that today of a Hitler who died in 1938?

We are inclined to say no for two reasons.

The first is that by 1938 Hitler had already decided on a war in which he would have to stake all his past achievements. Hitler wanted the war as early as September 1938, and in his reflections dictated to Bormann in February 1945 he still regretted not having started it then: 'From a military point of view we had an interest in starting it [the war] a year earlier ... but I could not do anything since the British and French accepted all my demands at Munich.' And as early as November 1938 he had admitted, in an address to the editors-in-chief of the domestic press, that all his promises of peace during the preceding years had been deception:

Circumstances compelled me to speak of almost nothing but peace for years on end. Only by continually emphasizing Germany's wish for peace and its peaceful intentions was I able to give the German people ... the rearmament that was necessary, time and again, as a prerequisite of the next step. It is obvious that such peace propaganda, conducted year after year, also has its problem side; it can all too easily result in the idea taking root in the brains of many people that the present regime as such identifies itself with the resolution and the will

41

to preserve peace under all circumstances. But that would lead not only to a wrong assessment of the goals of this system but, above all, it would lead to a situation in which the German nation was imbued with a spirit which, in the long run, would become defeatism and would liquidate, and be bound to liquidate, the very successes of the present regime.

Somewhat tortuously expressed but clear enough. Uncoded it means that for years on end he had been deceiving not only the foreign world but the Germans themselves with his speeches about peace. And the Germans had believed him; their revisionist hopes had been satisfied; in 1939 they did not, as they did in 1914, go to war with enthusiasm but with bewilderment and dejection. At least half the effect of Hitler's achievements during the years from 1933 to 1938 had been due precisely to the circumstance that they had been accomplished without war. Had the Germans known that these achievements had always only served the preparation for a war, many of them might well have thought differently about them, and even if they had discovered it only later (historiography could have hardly failed to make the discovery), would Hitler still have appeared to them as one of the greatest Germans?

It might be useful to continue Fest's speculative experiment also in another direction. Certainly, at the news of Hitler's sudden death in the autumn of 1938 most Germans would at first have felt that they had lost one of their greatest statesmen. But that feeling would probably have persisted for no more than a few weeks, because then they would have all discovered to their horror that they no longer possessed a functioning state organism. By 1938 Hitler had very quietly dismantled it.

How would things have continued? In 1938 Hitler had no successor, and there was no constitution in accordance with which a successor could have been elected, or an institution possessing the unquestioned right and unquestioned power to produce one. The Weimar constitution had long been invalid but it had never been replaced by another. The state, in consequence, lacked the organs through which it might have given itself a new head. The possible successors all derived their support from a state within the state – Goering from the Luftwaffe, Himmler from the ss, Hess from the Party (which, on that occasion, would have revealed itself as having virtually lost its functions just as much as the sa); in addition there was still the Army whose leading generals had quite recently, in September 1938, been all but ready to stage a coup. All in all, a political chaos held together and concealed by the person of Hitler, and bound to be mercilessly uncovered with the disappearance of that person. And that chaos was Hitler's creation, and if one wishes to put it that way his achievement, a destructive achievement that has so far been scarcely noted because it was finally swamped by a much more extensive destruction.

In our consideration of Hitler's life we have already encountered the somewhat monstrous fact that he subordinated his political timetable to his personal expectation of life. Now we are faced, from a totally different direction, with something similar – that he deliberately destroyed the state's ability to function in favour of his personal omnipotence and irreplaceability, and that he did so right from the start. A state's ability to function is based upon its constitution, whether written or unwritten. The Third Reich, however, had neither had a written nor an unwritten constitution from (at the latest) the autumn of 1934. It neither recognized nor respected any specific rights restricting the power of the state *vis-à-vis* the citizen, nor did it possess even the indispensable minimum of a constitution, i.e. procedural rules for the state that would define the rights of the various state authorities with regard to each other and ensure that their activities were meaningfully integrated. Hitler, on the contrary, had deliberately brought about a state of affairs in which the most various autonomous authorities were ranged alongside and against one another, without defined boundaries, in competition, and overlapping – and only he himself was at the head of all of them. Only thus was he able to secure for himself the completely unrestricted freedom of action which he intended to have in all directions. For he had the entirely proper understanding that any constitutional system must restrict the power of even the most powerful constitutional body. At the least, even the most powerful man in a constitutional state runs up against competences. He cannot order anybody to do anything, and arrangements exist to ensure that life can continue even without him. Hitler wanted none of this, and that was why he abolished what constitution there was without replacing it. He did not wish to be the first servant of the state but *Der Führer*, an absolute master. And he perceived correctly that absolute rule was not possible in an intact state organism but only amidst controlled chaos. That was why, from the outset, he replaced the state by chaos – and one has to hand it to him that, while he was alive, he knew how to control it. However, his death, even at the peak of his success, in the autumn of 1938, would have revealed the chaos he had created and, in consequence, surely after all compromised his posthumous fame.

There was something else that led Hitler to the wrecking of the state. A close study of him reveals a trait in him that one might describe as a horror of committing himself, or perhaps, even better, as a horror of anything final. It seems as though something within him caused him to recoil not only from setting limits to his power by way of a state system, but also to his will by way of a firm set of goals. The German Reich which he took over, and even the Greater German Reich into which he extended it in 1938, was to him never anything that he had to consolidate and preserve but always only a springboard towards a totally different, very much greater Reich. This would possibly no longer be a *German* Reich at all but a 'Greater Germanic' Reich, an empire to which he did not even set geographical bounds in his mind but only a continually advancing 'military boundary' which might perhaps find its final place on the Volga, perhaps along the Urals, or perhaps only on the Pacific. When, in his speech of 28 April 1939, repeatedly quoted above, he boasted that he had 'restored the thousand-year-old historical unity of German living space' he did not spell out his real thoughts: the 'living space' he was aiming at was far to the east, and it was not historical but futuristic. His

44

speech of 10 November 1938, which we have also quoted above, came nearer to providing a glimpse of his real thinking when he referred to 'time and again the next step' for which the German people would have to be psychologically prepared. But if each step was to be only a preparation for the next, then there was no reason to stop anywhere or to consolidate what had been achieved in the form of a durable state. On the contrary, what was solid would have to be made flexible and set in motion. Everything would have to be placed on a temporary footing, and from that temporary footing it would tend quite automatically towards continuous change, extension, enlargement. The German Reich had to cease to be a state in order to become fully an instrument of conquest.

In that respect there could be no greater contrast than between Hitler and Bismarck, who became a paragon of peace as soon as he had attained what had been attainable. Comparison with Napoleon is also instructive. Napoleon like Hitler failed as a conqueror, but much of what Napoleon achieved as a French statesman has been preserved. His great legislative work, his educational system, indeed his taut administrative structure with its Département Prefects exists to this day as he created it, in spite of all the changes in state form that have occurred since. Hitler did not create any state edifice, and his achievements, which for ten years overwhelmed the Germans and made the world hold its breath, have proved ephemeral and have left no trace, not only because they ended in disaster but because they were never designed for endurance. As a star performer Hitler probably ranks even higher than Napoleon. But one thing he never was – a statesman.

Successes

THE graph of Hitler's successes presents a riddle similar to the graph of his life. This, as the reader will remember, revealed an unexplained but marked jump from total inactivity and obscurity during the first thirty years to public activity on the largest possible scale during the next twenty-six. His line of successes actually shows two such jumps. All Hitler's successes fall within a span of twelve years, 1930 to 1941. Previously, he had been consistently unsuccessful in a political career which, after all, had been going on for ten years. His putsch in 1923 had failed, and his party, newly founded in 1925, had remained an insignificant splinter party until 1929. After 1941, indeed from the autumn of 1941 onwards, there were again no more successes. His military enterprises failed, defeat piled on defeat, his allies abandoned him, the coalition of his enemies held together. The end is well known. But from 1930 until 1941 Hitler succeeded in practically everything he undertook, in domestic and foreign politics and eventually also in the military field, to the amazement of the world.

Let us look at the chronology: 1930, votes gained in the Reichstag elections octupled; 1932, doubled again; January 1933, Hitler Reich Chancellor, all rival parties dissolved in July; 1934, Hitler as Reich President and Supreme Commander of the Reichswehr; total power. After that there was nothing more left for him to gain at home. Now began the series of foreign policy successes: 1935, general conscription in breach of the Versailles Peace Treaty – and nothing happened; 1936, remilitarization of the Rhineland in breach of the Treaty of Locarno – and nothing happened; March 1938, Austria incorporated – and nothing happened; September, Sudeten territories incorporated – and with the express agreement of France and Britain; March 1939, Protectorate of Bohemia and Moravia; occupation of Memel. This completes the series of foreign policy successes. From then onward Hitler ran into opposition. And now begin the military successes: September 1939, Poland defeated; 1940, Denmark, Norway, Hol-

49

land, Belgium and Luxembourg occupied, France defeated; 1941, Yugoslavia and Greece occupied. Hitler dominated the continent of Europe.

All in all ten years of failure followed by twelve years of unbroken giddy success, then again four years of failure ending in catastrophe. And between each of those phases a clear break.

No matter how long one searches, one will not find anything comparable in history. Rise and fall, certainly; alternation of success and failure, certainly. But never three such clear-cut periods of pure failure, pure success, and again pure failure. On no other occasion did the same person first prove himself for a protracted period a seemingly hopeless bungler, then for an equally long period a seemingly inspired performer, and then again, this time not just seemingly, a hopeless bungler. This calls for an explanation. And it cannot be explained in terms of those obvious parallels for which one instinctively reaches.

Certainly, not all politicians are equally good all the time; nearly all of them make occasional mistakes which they subsequently patch up as best they can. That is a familiar picture. One also knows that many politicians need a certain period of apprenticeship and getting into their stride before reaching the peak of their form, and that on that peak they will tire or slacken after a certain time or, alternatively, become reckless and overplay their hand. All these obvious attempted explanations simply do not fit in Hitler's case. They do not explain the two sudden breaks between prolonged success and prolonged failure. Nor can these be explained by changes in Hitler's character or by any growth or decline of his abilities. Hitler always remained the same.

He certainly was not one of those (by no means rare) figures of history who, having achieved success, lose the qualities to which they owed their success. There is no question of Hitler ever having become self-indulgent, having relaxed the reins or having relinquished them. His energy and resolution were equally stupendous from the first to the last day of his public activity, and his rule, even in the bunker of the Reich Chancellory to which his territory had ultimately shrunk, was absolute. When one of the occupants of that bunker, Eva Braun's brother-in-law Fegelein, tried to make off on 28 April 1945, two days before Hitler's suicide, and Hitler thereupon gave orders for him to be brought back and to be shot, he was brought back and shot. That order was as characteristic as its prompt execution. The unsuccessful Hitler of the last four years of the war was the same Hitler as the successful man of the preceding years; the fact that he was taking pills, that he found it difficult to sleep or that he occasionally suffered from a tremor in his arms did not in the least impair his resolution to have his will and see it implemented. Accounts presenting Hitler during the final years of the war as a mere shadow of himself, a pitiable human wreck, are all hopelessly overdrawn. Hitler's disastrous failures from 1941 to 1945, following the preceding twelve years of successes, cannot be explained by physical or mental decline.

Nor can it be explained – and this has also been attempted, sometimes in the same breath as the contradictory thesis of his alleged physical decline – by hubris, by the megalomania of a man pampered by success recklessly challenging fate. Hitler's decision to attack Russia, which marked the beginning of his decline, was not the fruit of recent recklessness born of success. It had for many years been Hitler's well-considered and chosen main goal, laid down and justified in *Mein Kampf* as early as 1926. The other disastrous decision of 1941, the declaration of war on America, sprang if anything from a moment of despair rather than recklessness (we shall deal with it in detail in the chapter 'Mistakes'). And the stubbornness with which Hitler in failure clung to his chosen course was the same stubbornness he had shown in failure during the years 1925 to 1929, when, in spite of all efforts, his party was getting no nearer to its objective of a 'legal' seizure of power. If Hitler was a megalomaniac – and in a certain sense he can be so described – then he was one from the start. What could have been more 'megalomaniacal' than the decision of an unknown failure to become a politician? Hitler repeatedly said himself that compared with the daring of his beginnings anything afterwards had been child's play; and one may believe him on this point. Besides, his 'years of apprenticeship' as a politician had been exceptionally short, if indeed one may speak of years of apprenticeship at all. Strictly speaking, the failure of his putsch in 1923 was the only thing he ever learned a lesson from. For the rest he always remained the same, in a downright uncanny way. His policy, at least from 1925 to 1945, was entirely of one cast. What changed twice during those twenty years was the strength of opposition that it encountered.

And this suddenly gives us the key to the secret of Hitler's graph of success. That key lies not in any changes in Hitler. It lies in the change and alternation of the opponents with whom Hitler had to deal.

We have deliberately made a distinction between Hitler's achievements and his successes. Achievements belong to one person. Successes always involve two – and the success of the one is the failure of the other. Given constant strength one can be successful against a weaker opponent and unsuccessful against a stronger one – a platitude. But platitudes so often tend to be disregarded. If we refuse to disregard it in this instance we shall find everything explained. Hitler's successes and failures become instantly explicable if one turns one's attention away from Hitler and towards his opponents at the times in question.

The point is that Hitler's successes were never scored against a strong or even a tough opponent: even the Weimar Republic of the late twenties and Britain in 1940 proved too strong for him. More particularly, he never possessed the inventiveness or suppleness which may enable a weaker contestant to outmanoeuvre and defeat a stronger one. In his struggle against the allied coalition of 1942 to 1945 he never showed even the glimmer of an idea of exploiting the internal tensions of the coalition with a view to splitting it apart. On the contrary, Hitler more than anyone else contributed to the conclusion of the (in many respects unnatural) wartime coalition of West and East, and his blind stubbornness did a lot to hold it together even though it was occasionally creaking at the joints.

All his successes were scored against opponents who were unable or unwilling to offer real resistance. At home he dealt the *coup de grâce* to the Weimar Republic when it had already been undermined and practically given up. Externally he finished off the European peace system of 1919 when it had already been shaken from within and had proved itself to be untenable. In both instances Hitler overthrew something that was collapsing already.

Furthermore, in the thirties, unlike the twenties and the forties, Hitler was dealing with weak opponents throughout, in terms of personalities. The German conservatives themselves who for a while challenged his succession to the Weimar Republic lacked a political concept, were divided amongst themselves and psychologically vacillated between resistance to and alliance with Hitler. The British and French statesmen of the late thirties, against whom Hitler scored his foreign policy successes, similarly vacillated between resistance and alliance. If one looks more closely at the condition of Germany in 1930, of Europe in 1935, and of France in 1940, Hitler's successes begin to lose the halo of the miraculous which they had for his contemporaries. We must make the effort to take that closer look, even though these reflections will seem at times to lead us away from Hitler. But without a little contemporary history Hitler's successes remain incomprehensible.

By 1930 the Weimar Republic was finished even before Hitler scored his first great electoral success in September. The Brüning government, formed in March, was the first of those presidential Cabinets which were to make the transition to an entirely different state and constitutional system, even though that system had not been thought out or defined in detail. Unlike his two successors Papen and Schleicher, Brüning still adhered to constitutional legality – the 'emergency decrees' by means of which he governed were still 'tolerated' by the Reichstag – but Brüning no longer had a parliamentary majority behind him, as demanded by the constitution. By means of the fiction of a permanent state of emergency, which permitted him to govern without the Reichstag, he had already invalidated the Weimar constitution in practice. It is therefore a misconception, though a widespread one, that the Weimar Republic was toppled by Hitler's assault. It was already toppling when Hitler seriously stepped upon the scene, and the domestic political struggles of the period from 1930 to 1934 were in reality no longer about the defence of the Republic but solely about its succession. The only question was whether the Republic, already given up, should be replaced by a conservative – in ultimate logic probably monarchist – restoration or by Hitler.

To understand this starting point one has to cast a brief glance at the history of the Weimar Republic, an unhappy history from the start.

At its foundation the Republic was supported only by a left-of-centre three-party coalition, the Social Democrats, the Left liberals and the Catholics, a grouping which had already represented the majority in the Reichstag during the final years of Imperial Germany and which, at the last moment of the Empire, in October 1918, had achieved (or rather had been saddled with) its transformation into a parliamentary state. After the revolution of November 1918 it formed the 'Weimar Coalition' of the National Assembly, created the Weimar constitution which was essentially modelled on that of the parliamentarized German Empire, and started to govern. But after a single year, in the first republican Reichstag elections, it lost its parliamentary majority and never again regained it.

Before that there had been the unscheduled revolution of November 1918. This had not suited the plans of the Weimar coalition in the least and had been crushed by it. That in turn had given rise to a disappointed and embittered permanent opposition from the Left which had never accepted the Weimar state and never reconciled itself with it. But the revolution at least had produced *one* result that could not be reversed – the abolition of the monarchy. So the Weimar coalition had no choice but to make the republic created by the revolution its own. By doing that it gave rise to an even more numerous and powerful permanent opposition from the Right, which did not accept the Weimar Republic, 'the state of the November revolution', any more than did the disappointed Left revolutionaries. At the same time it was more dangerous than the Left-wing opposition because it continued to occupy virtually all senior posts in the Army and in the civil service; the Weimar state thus had a whole army of enemies of the constitution in its own public service from the very start. From 1920 onwards, moreover, the Right-wing and Left-wing opponents of the Republic together had a majority in the Reichstag, and by 1925 the Republic, though barely launched, had been lurching for years like a ship in distress. Hardly a year passed without some putsch from the Right or the Left. (Hitler's putsch of 1923 was one of many.) No one would at that time have predicted a long life for the Republic.

And yet it was granted a brief period of seeming consolidation, the 'Golden Twenties', the years from 1925 to 1929. These were for Hitler the years of total eclipse, when his blustering hostility to the Republic produced virtually no echo and was beginning to look ludicrous. What had changed? What made the 'Republic without republicans' suddenly viable?

Several things. A capable Foreign Minister, Gustav Stresemann, was achieving some steps towards conciliation with Germany's wartime enemies, as well as various alleviations and small prestige successes. American credits were ensuring a modest economic boom. Most important of all, the massive and powerful Right-wing opposition, always (or still) firmly anchored in all the Ministries and authorities of the state it rejected, had temporarily and experimentally abandoned its opposition to that state and condescended to govern it. The enemies of the Republic had, for a few years, turned into 'republicans of expedience'.

The decisive event which made that half-change of opinion possible and gave the Republic its chance of consolidation was Hindenburg's election as Reich President in April 1925. This has often been seen as the beginning of the end of the Republic. Totally wrong. Hindenburg's election was a piece of luck for the Republic and gave it the only chance it ever had. With the war hero and the Kaiser's field-marshal at its head the Republic suddenly appeared presentable to the Right which until then had firmly rejected it. Something like a conciliation began to take shape. This lasted from 1925 to 1928 while a Centre–Right coalition of Catholics, Right-wing liberals and conservatives formed the Reich Government. Thus the state-supporting party system was temporarily broadened, for the first and only time, to comprise the full width of the Right–Left spectrum, with the exception of radical fringe groups such as Communists and National Socialists; the Social Democrats' and Left-wing liberals' loyalty to the state, though they were now in opposition, was in any case beyond doubt.

But that remained an episode. When the Right-wing government lost the elections in 1928 and when, for the first time since 1920, a Social Democrat again became Reich Chancellor, it was all over again. Under a new leader, Hugenberg, the conservatives once more swung briskly to an anti-Republican course. Even the Catholic Centre, likewise under a new leader, Kaas, was talking about the need for an authoritarian regime; and in the Reichswehr Ministry a politically ambitious general, von Schleicher, was beginning to make plans for a *coup d'état*. It was decided that it must never again be possible for the Right to suffer anything like the electoral defeat of 1928; the government, a perpetual Right-wing government, was to be made independent of Parliament and elections, just as in Bismarck's empire; parliamentary government was to be scrapped, a presidential regime was to be installed.

The moment came in March 1930. Stresemann had died in October 1929. That same month a collapse on the American Stock Exchange ushered in a world-wide depression which instantly had disastrous effects in Germany. The government had been unable to adjust to it and had resigned, but this time it was not replaced by another parliamentary government. Instead, a little-known right-of-centre figure, Brüning (Schleicher's candidate), became Reich Chancellor without a parliamentary majority but with quasi-dictatorial powers and with the secret task of performing the transition to a conservative-authoritarian regime, independent of Parliament. Meanwhile he was governing by means of emergency decrees under the emergency regulations, and when the Reichstag would no longer play ball he dissolved it. That was Hitler's opportunity. In the intact (or seemingly intact) republic of the period from 1925 to 1929 there had been nothing for him to do. In the political crisis of 1930 his party at a stroke became the second strongest.

Hitler at the gate! From that moment onwards even the Social Democrats tolerated Brüning's unparliamentary emergency regime as the lesser evil, and for nearly two years Brüning managed to continue to govern semi-legally. But the Depression got worse and the wave of Hitlerism rose with it, and, moreover, Brüning did not find the way from his semi-legal form of government to the new authoritarian state for which Schleicher had instructed him to prepare the ground. He was therefore overthrown in May 1932. A new candidate of Schleicher's, von Papen, with even less support in Parliament, became Reich Chancellor, formed a 'Cabinet of Barons' and proclaimed 'an entirely new type of state government'. As a first step he again dissolved the Reichstag, and Hitler's party promptly doubled its seats once more and became the strongest party. From that moment onwards there was only the alternative Papen/Schleicher or Hitler. No one was talking about a parliamentary Republic any longer. It had already been tacitly buried. The struggle was about the succession.

In that exciting game of intrigue between Papen/Schleicher and Hitler, which occupied the months from August 1932 until January 1933 and which need not be recounted here in detail, it was clear from the outset that Hitler held the stronger cards if only for the simple reason that he was *one* and his opponents were *two*. Also, he had a mass movement behind him while Papen and Schleicher only had the unharnessed élite of the defunct German Empire. But most of all he knew exactly what he wanted, whereas Papen and Schleicher did not – and indeed *could* not know it. The one thing that could have given their authoritarian state a backbone, certainly after the end of the 85-year-old Hindenburg, would have been the restoration of the monarchy. But that they dared not openly envisage, and with good reason, for there was no suitable or credible candidate for the throne. So they got entangled in impossible speculations. Papen – that dashing gentleman rider – dreamed of a ban on all political parties and of a pure upper-class or indeed aristocratic dictatorship based upon nothing but the bayonets of the Reichswehr. Schleicher, who (more realistically) thought that this would be too much to ask of the Reichswehr, had equally fantastic dreams, a split of the National Socialists and a coalition of 'moderate' Nazis (without Hitler), trade unions, youth leagues and Reichswehr as the foundation of a Fascist corporate state. Needless to say, both of them failed before they had properly begun, but the most important result of that failure was that they quarrelled over it. Schleicher overthrew Papen and made himself Reich Chancellor. And Papen, thirsting for revenge and always ready for a gamble, thereupon allied himself with Hitler against Schleicher and persuaded Hindenburg to drop Schleicher and appoint Hitler Reich Chancellor. He had always been prepared to accept Hitler as a junior partner (once more, in a sense, as the 'drummer'); now he was prepared to play the part of junior partner to Reich Chancellor Hitler. He was still hoping to 'box him in' with his aristocratic conservative ministerial crew.

But that plan did not work out. How Hitler outplayed his conservative junior partner during the next few months, and finally in the following year, until, after Hindenburg's death in August 1934, total power was concentrated in his hands – all that is too well known to require a detailed account. What does deserve being recorded, because it is by no means generally known – indeed it may come as a surprise to many – is this: The only opponents or rivals whom Hitler had to consider seriously and whom at times he had to fight in the domestic political arena between 1930 and 1934, were the conservatives. The liberals, the Centre people or the Social Democrats never gave him the least trouble, and neither did the communists.

And this is how things remained throughout the years of his unlimited power following 1934. The liberals, Centre people and Social Democrats, if they remained faithful to their convictions, almost entirely withdrew into the passivity of an inner emigration, innocuous to Hitler, or of external emigration; and the purely symbolical resistance and underground cohesion of small communist groups, time and again busted and time and again reformed, though demanding respect for their death-defying hopelessness, were merely a police problem to Hitler. But the conservatives, with their well dug-in positions in army, diplomatic service and administration, always remained to him a genuine political problem – indispensable for day-to-day operation, half allies but always also half opponents and occasionally, at least some of them, total opponents. Papen and Schleicher once more became active during the crisis of the summer of 1934 (Schleicher paid for this with his life while Papen was shunted to diplomatic posts abroad); conservative Wehrmacht generals still plotted coups in 1938 and 1939; conservative politicians such as Goerdeler and Popitz conspired against Hitler throughout the whole war with the most varied of partners from the Army, the state and economic life. By 1944 something like a grand coalition of political and military conservative opponents to Hitler had taken shape, culminating in the attempt on his life on 20 July. This attempt was essentially a conservative enterprise and it has rightly been observed that its casualty list reads like an excerpt from the Almanach de Gotha, even though a few youngish Social Democratic politicians had been envisaged, for appearance's sake, for a few ministerial posts in the planned putsch government. The attempt failed largely because the romantic–conservative political ideas which it tried to realize were just as undigested, anachronistic and removed from reality as Papen's and Schleicher's concepts of the state had been.

The conservative opposition never managed to become really dangerous to Hitler, and the string of his easy successes against it was never-ending. Nevertheless it was the only opposition that troubled him right to the end; the only one which stood any chance at all, however slight, of toppling him, and which, on one occasion at least, made the attempt to do so. And that opposition came from the Right. From its point of view Hitler stood on the Left.

That should give one pause. Hitler can by no means be placed so readily on the extreme Right in the political spectrum as many people nowadays are fond of doing. Of course he was no democrat but he was a populist, a man who based his power on the masses, not on the élite, and in a sense a people's tribune risen to absolute power. His principal means of rule was demagogy, and his instrument of government was not a structured hierarchy but a chaotic bundle of unco-ordinated mass organizations merely held together at the top by his own person. All these are 'Leftist' rather than 'Rightist' features.

Clearly, in the line of twentieth-century dictators Hitler stands somewhere between Mussolini and Stalin, and upon closer examination nearer to Stalin than to Mussolini. Nothing is more misleading than to call Hitler a Fascist. Fascism is upper-class rule, buttressed by artificially manufactured mass enthusiasm. Certainly Hitler roused masses to enthusiasm, but never in order to buttress an upper class. He was not a class politician, and his National Socialism was anything but Fascism. We already noted in the preceding chapter that his 'socialization of the human being' has exact parallels in such socialist countries as the present-day Soviet Union and GDR, parallels which in Fascist states are, at best, poorly developed and frequently totally lacking. Of course, Hitler's 'National Socialism' differed from Stalin's 'socialism in one country' (note the terminological identity!) through the continuing existence of the private ownership of the means of production – a vital difference in Marxist eyes. But whether in a totalitarian dictatorial state such as Hitler's that difference is really so vital is open to question. The differences from Mussolini's classical Fascism certainly are more vital: no monarchy, hence no possibility of sacking or exchanging the dictator; no rigid hierarchy in party or state; no constitution (not even a Fascist one); no real alliance with the traditional upper classes, least of all any subservience to them. One outward detail was symbolical for much that was essential: Mussolini wore a tail-coat as often as a party uniform. Hitler wore tails only occasionally during the transitional period 1933/34, while Hindenburg was still Reich President and Hitler still had to keep up his apparent alliance with Papen. After that he always only wore uniform, like Stalin. One last brief reflection arises before we turn from Hitler's domestic successes of the years 1930–34 to his foreign policy successes of 1935–38, which are just as easily explained by contemporary history. People often ask: would a Hitler stand the same chance as in 1930 if he emerged in the German Federal Republic today, especially if economic depression and unemployment were to assume similar proportions to those in the Weimar Republic at the time? If our analysis of Hitler's seizure of power is correct then the answer is reassuring. No, Hitler would not stand the same chance, for the simple reason that in the Federal Republic there is no state-rejecting Right wing that might be prepared to destroy the state in preparation for him.

After all, a state does not simply fall apart as a result of depression and mass unemployment, otherwise, for instance, America with its thirteen million unemployed during the Great Depression of 1930–33 would have crumbled. The Weimar Republic was not destroyed by economic depression or unemployment, though these naturally contributed to the atmosphere of doom, but because the Weimar Right had long been resolved to abolish the parliamentary state in favour of a vaguely conceived authoritarian state. Nor was it destroyed by Hitler. He already found it destroyed when he became Reich Chancellor, and he merely stripped those who had destroyed it of their power.

The great difference between Bonn and Weimar, however, is quite simply the fact that in the Federal Republic the political force which wrecked the Weimar Republic, i.e. a state-rejecting Right wing, no longer exists. Perhaps it is just its defeat in its rivalry with Hitler, and the bitter and at times bloody lesson of its many years of unsuccessful attempted opposition to him, that has converted the German Right to the Republic, to parliamentarianism and to democracy. At any rate it has learned since Hitler that it will do better, as a parliamentary party, to pit itself against other, Left-wing, parliamentary parties in the tug-of-war of government and opposition than to compete with a populist-demagogical dictator for the leadership of an authoritarian state. The foundation of the CDU, an amalgamation of the Catholic Centre Party with the former Right-wing parties, characterizes that fundamental change of attitude of the Right and is just as much an epoch-making event in German politics as the transformation of the Social Democratic Party from a revolutionary into a parliamentary party had been thirty years earlier. The Federal Republic possesses what the Weimar Republic did not – a democratic Right. As a state it is supported not merely by a Centre–Left coalition but by the entire party spectrum (always excluding radical fringe groups). Thus events such as the ones which cleared the road for Hitler in 1930 are not to be expected again as far as is humanly predictable. Bonn, by its very political structure and not simply because of some superiority of the Bonn Basic Law (*Grundgesetz*) over the Weimar constitution, is a more solid and stronger democratic state than Weimar was; and – our final observation on this subject – it will remain so even if, as indeed during its first seventeen years, it should one day have a Right-wing government again and even if, for instance as a response to terrorism, it should tighten up its laws. Those who, on these grounds, are comparing the German Federal Republic with Hitler's Reich – almost exclusively people who did not experience Hitler themselves – do not know what they are talking about.

Enough, then, of Hitler's domestic successes and on to those of his foreign policy, which likewise he owed more to the weakness of his opponents than to his own strength. Just as at home, in 1930, he already found the republic of 1919 on its deathbed, so in the foreign policy field of 1935 he found the European system of 1919 in an advanced state of disintegration. Just as he had done at home, he now also found the foreign supporters of the *status quo* already dispirited, and among those who wanted to replace it by something else he found involuntary helpers. To understand why this should have been so we have to cast a brief retrospective glance, similar to the one on the history of the Weimar Republic, at the history of the European peace system created in Paris in 1919.

It is an equally unhappy story and it even has the same structure. The Paris peace system suffered from the same congenital weakness as the Weimar Republic. Just as the Republic suffered shipwreck because, from the outset, it failed either to strip the German Right wing (still the strongest power group and one that was indispensable to the functioning of the state) of its power for good (which it would have had the opportunity of doing after the 1918 revolution) or permanently to integrate it into the new republican state, so the Paris peace system foundered because it neither stripped the still strongest European power, the German Reich (still indispensable to European stability), permanently of its power, nor permanently integrated it. Its creators, in point of fact, did the opposite in both courses of action. Instead of enlisting Germany from the start as a participant in the creation of the peace system, as Metternich had done with France following the Napoleonic Wars, they humiliated it and put it in the pillory. And instead, as would then have been consistent, of making it permanently incapable of disturbing the peace, for instance by partition or occupation, they allowed it not only to keep its unity and independence, which had made it the strongest power in Europe from 1871 to 1918, but, without clearly realizing what they were doing, even enlarged that power by extensively abolishing such counterweights as had previously existed.

It is psychologically understandable that the Treaty of Versailles – that part of the Paris peace arrangement of 1919 which directly concerned Germany – had been regarded by Germany as the insult which in fact it was. The insult lay principally in the manner of its imposition. The Treaty really was just what the insulted Germans called it – a *Diktat*, a dictated peace. It was not, as other European peace treaties in the past had been, negotiated and agreed between victors and vanquished. In such treaties, of course, the negotiating position of the victors would be the stronger but the participation of the vanquished was at least formally equal, thus preserving their honour and morally underpinning their share in the responsibility for the observ-

63

ance of the agreed terms. In the Treaty of Versailles the German signature under what had been negotiated and agreed without German participation was enforced by an ultimatum under the threat of war. This ensured from the start that the Germans did not feel bound by what they had signed under duress, and even without the numerous humiliating, discriminating, or simply irritating detailed stipulations with which the Treaty abounded they would have been confirmed in their intention 'to shake off the fetters of Versailles'. That intention determined Germany's entire foreign policy from 1919 to 1939, under Weimar as much as under Hitler. And the Weimar Republic scored certain successes just as Hitler did. Hitler found the peace system, of which 'the fetters of Versailles' formed one part, already in full dissolution.

Those fetters of Versailles, as had already been proved, even before Hitler ripped off the last of them with stunning effortlessness, were made of paper. On paper the incorporation of Austria, desired by both parties, was forbidden, as were modern weapons for the German armed forces. On paper these armed forces were limited to 100,000 men; and on paper Germany was obliged to pay reparations for several generations to come. But the power to enforce these paper limitations and obligations did not exist. The decisions of the Paris Peace Conference of 1919 had seen to that. Indeed – a point initially missed in Germany under the shock of the insult and only gradually recognized – they had achieved precisely that which Germany in four years of war effort had failed to achieve – to make Germany the absolute, irresistible leading power in Europe. The territorial amputations performed on its geographical body did not change that fact.

What had prevented Germany, from 1871 until 1914, from developing its position as the strongest single power in Europe into an absolute position of hegemony had been her close proximity to four other European great powers: Britain, France, Austria-Hungary and Russia, great powers which had to be considered because, though Germany was stronger than any one of them, it was naturally weaker than all of them combined. And what, from 1914 to 1918, had prevented its 'reaching out for world power' had been a grand coalition of Britain and France, first with Russia and then with America. Of the four pre-war European great powers one, Austria-Hungary, was destroyed in Paris in 1919 and another, Russia, was excluded from any co-operation in Europe. Russia, in consequence, had also been excluded from the victorious coalition; and America, which in 1917 had leaped into the breach left by Russia, at the same time withdrew from the victorious coalition and refused to take part in the peace arrangements of its former allies. Those peace arrangements were, in consequence, virtually underpinned only by Britain and France, just as the Weimar Republic had been underpinned only by the three parties of the Weimar coalition. In both cases the basis was too narrow to carry the load. The German Reich, which had been preserved in its substance – a glance at the course of the First World War will confirm this – was too strong in the long run to be kept in check by Britain and France alone. And the newly created small states which now occupied the territory of the former Austria-Hungary and the area between Germany and Russia were almost predestined to become German satellites as soon as Germany recovered from the excessive strain of the war and the shock of defeat. In Paris Germany had not only, by humiliating treatment, been driven on to the road of revisionism and re-vanchism but this road had been almost obsessively smoothed for her as much as possible.

The two powers responsible for that, Britain and France, very soon dimly realized that they had made a capital mistake. But from that incipient realization they drew opposite conclusions. Britain thought it had to appease Germany by a gradual alleviation of the peace terms and eventually to turn an implacable enemy into a willing co-supporter of such a revised peace arrangement, whereas France, on the contrary, believed that the omissions of Paris would have to be made good and Germany now truly stripped of all power. The conflict erupted openly when France actually attempted to do this by occupying the Ruhr territory in 1923. Britain did not join in, France had to yield, and henceforward, quietly gnashing its teeth, followed the British policy of 'appeasement'. That appeasement did not start, as the legend has it, at Munich in 1938, under Neville Chamberlain – if anything it ended there – but at Locarno in 1925 under his half-brother Austen Chamberlain.

The period which followed, associated in Germany mainly with the name of Stresemann, is a strangely accurate companion piece in the international field to the domestic German period following Hindenburg's election with which it also, initially, coincided. However, it outlasted it since even Brüning, Papen and Schleicher all continued to sail in the wake of British appeasement, and even Hitler himself did so for the first five years – at least seemingly. Just as in Germany the Right-wing opponents of the Republic agreed for a while to accept the Republic, provided they were allowed to govern it, so Germany for a while agreed to respect the Paris peace arrangements, provided these were dismantled piece by piece.

And they were dismantled. The successes of Stresemann, Brüning, Papen and Schleicher were no less than Hitler's. They include the Locarno Treaty, Germany's admission to the League of Nations, the pre-term evacuation of the occupied Rhineland, the scrapping of reparations, and the recognition in principle of Germany's equal right to rearmament. Hitler's successes – rearmament and general conscription, the naval treaty with Britain, remilitarization of the Rhineland, the incorporation of Austria, the incorporation of the Sudeten area – have a point of difference with them. Hitler's predecessors made a particular point of emphasizing each time the conciliatory character of each success in order to keep Britain sweet and its policy of appeasement in existence. Hitler, on the other hand, attached the greatest importance to making his successes appear as having been wrested from a hostile world. What is more, he succeeded in this, not only because of his total control of German public opinion but also because of a certain predisposition of that German public mood which had always hoped for just such triumphs of truculence against the hated system of Versailles, and which had only been half as happy about foreign policy successes accomplished in the name of conciliation. But by the manner in which he stage-managed the foreign policy successes he had been allowed or even encouraged to score, Hitler progressively irritated his British partners. They could not fail to notice that he was increasingly withholding from them the hoped-for collateral, participation in the consolidation of peace in Europe and shared support for a peace system revised in Germany's favour. Indeed, they gradually began to suspect – and with very good reason – that everything they had allowed him to win for the purpose of consolidating peace he had in reality accepted to increase his strength for a new war. Even the incorporation of Austria had been accepted by Britain without the batting of an eyelid; but when he proceeded to absorb the Sudeten areas Britain wanted to have a say, and the Munich Agreement in which it once more conceded this 'last territorial demand' of Hitler already caused great controversy in Britain. When, six months later, Hitler broke that agreement by marching into Prague everything was over. Appeasement was buried and replaced, even and especially in Britain, by a grimly resigned resolve to risk a new war with Germany.

Seen in that light it is almost doubtful whether Hitler's foreign policy successes should properly still be described as pure successes or should not perhaps be listed under his mistakes, with which we shall deal in a later chapter. To say the least, they prepared the way for the big mistake Hitler made during 1939 to 1941 when he jeopardized Germany's no longer disputed hegemony in Europe by converting it into the military conquest and occupation of Europe, a step comparable to the deliberate rape of a woman perfectly willing to surrender.

Nevertheless, those years, too, still brought him certain successes – superfluous ones and, in the long run, even damaging ones, but successes for all that, though not of a political but a military nature. Among these successes only one was really impressive – the rapid and easy military victory over France. That

Germany should be able militarily to overwhelm such countries as Poland, Denmark, Norway, Holland, Belgium, Luxembourg, Yugoslavia and Greece, whenever she felt like it, surprised no one and aroused not admiration but fear and hatred. But that under Hitler's leadership she should reduce France, on which in the First World War she had broken her teeth for four years, in a mere six weeks confirmed once more, for the last time, Hitler's reputation as a miracle worker and this time also as a military genius. In the eyes of his admirers, after all his domestic and foreign policy successes he became, in 1940, also the 'greatest general of all time'.

That he was nothing of the kind need no longer be elaborately proved today. If anything, one has to defend him a little against his military critics. The German generals of the Second World War would all of them, according to their memoirs, have won the war if Hitler had not prevented them. But that was not the case either. Hitler certainly understood something of how to wage war. He had intellectually digested his front-line experiences of the First World War rather better than anything else, and had continued to work on his military knowledge after the war. By comparison with his opponents, Churchill, Roosevelt and Stalin – all of them similarly amateur strategists who understood their power of supreme command by no means purely nominally and often bossed their generals about – , he does not cut a poor figure in the military field; nor by comparison with some of his own generals. True, the idea of an independent armoured force originated with Guderian, and the brilliant strategic plan of the French campaign – a far better plan than the famous Schlieffen plan – was Manstein's work. But without Hitler neither Guderian nor Manstein would have prevailed against the high-ranking, more tradition-bound and often more blinkered army generals. It was Hitler who took up their plans and to whom they owed their realization. And if Hitler's unimaginative, stubborn and rigid defensive strategy in the latter years of the war in Russia all too clearly revealed his fixation upon the trench mentality of the First World War, one must ask oneself whether without Hitler's stubbornness the war in Russia might not perhaps have ended disastrously in its first winter. Hitler certainly was not the military genius he believed himself to be, but neither was he the hopeless military illiterate and bungler that is shown, in the role of scapegoat, in so many German generals' memoirs. The stunning military success of the campaign against France in 1940 must certainly be largely attributed to him.

And not only because he recognized the value of Manstein's plan of campaign and put it into effect against the reservations of the Commander-in-Chief of the Army, Brauchitsch, and the Chief of the General Staff, Halder, but mainly because he, and he alone, saw to it that the campaign was ventured upon at all. The German generals all had before their eyes the spectre of the French campaign of 1914 which, after the initial impetus, had got bogged down into four years of positional warfare. Rather than risk such an adventure for a second time many of them had even been prepared, in the winter of 1939, to stage a coup against Hitler. And, like the German generals, the whole world expected, as a matter of course, that France would repeat her miracle of defence of 1914 – all except Hitler that is. It was precisely that universal expectation and its rapid disappointment that made Hitler's victory over France appear in such a radiant light, like a genuine miracle. But it was nothing of the sort. The miracle had been France's defensive achievement in 1914; and the France of 1940 was not the France of 1914. (Perhaps it should also be pointed out that the France of 1978 is no longer the France of 1940. It is a physically and morally rejuvenated and reinvigorated nation.) France in 1940 was internally defeated before the first tanks crossed the Meuse.

During our account of the disintegration of the Paris peace system we tended to lose sight of France in 1924, the year when, following the failure of her unilateral action in the Ruhr, she inevitably aligned herself with the British policy of appeasement, at first reluctantly and trying to put brakes on it, later with increasing indifference and finally with an almost masochistic excess of zeal. Since that year France had in fact played a subordinate part in European politics. The protagonists had been Britain and Germany, and the question was whether British appeasement and German revisionism could be harmonized or not. All that France could do was hope for the best, i.e. that Germany would ultimately really be satisfied by the progressive reduction of her grievances.

If not, then things looked bad for France, since any concession to Germany was at France's expense. Each further concession restored the natural superiority of a nation of 70 millions over a nation of 40 millions, a superiority which France had in vain tried to break between 1919 and 1923. And if appeasement – as was always feared in France – would prove in vain and if Germany, strong again, were to turn to attack and revenge one day, then Britain at least had the sea between her and Germany. France now no longer even had the Rhine. France followed the British policy even though she assessed the chances of its success very pessimistically from the start. She tagged along because she had no choice. But her nerve was being broken by degrees in the process. Her will to assert herself was paralysed; she could no longer face a second battle of the Marne, a second Verdun. Ever since 1936, when Hitler with his forces had again moved into the old starting lines in the Rhineland – the same Rhineland which France had evacuated only six years previously as part of appeasement – France had been staring at Hitler's Germany as a rabbit stares at a snake. In the end she may have subconsciously positively desired the inevitable terrible end. 'Il faut en finir' – 'Let's get it over with' – that battle cry with which France went to war in 1939 almost had the ring of a call for defeat. Anything to get it over!

The history of France between 1919 and 1939, the history of a painfully won and subsequently totally lost victory and of a progressive descent from proudest self-confidence to almost accomplished self-surrender, is a tragedy. In Germany, needless to say, where France continued to be remembered as the malicious tormentor of the first few post-war years, it was not seen in that light. Or rather it was not seen at all. People believed they were still dealing not only with the triumphant France of 1919 but also with the heroic France of 1914. The German generals were nearly as much afraid of a new Marne and a new Verdun as the French. And not only the Germans. Astonishingly, the whole world, with Britain and Russia in the lead, based their calculations at the outbreak of war in 1939 almost as a matter of course upon a France which, at any time, as in 1914, would be prepared to shed the blood of her sons in rivers to defend her soil. Only Hitler did nothing of the kind.

In retrospect it is easy to see what only Hitler saw at the time: throughout fifteen years France had been acting against her own vital interests through a sense of resigned hopelessness. In 1925 she had concluded the Locarno Treaty by which she had virtually surrendered her small eastern allies; in 1930 she had evacuated the Rhineland where she could have remained for another five years; in 1932 she had renounced her reparation demands in the summer and in the autumn she had conceded equal military rights to Germany; in 1935 she had watched, as if mesmerized, Germany's massive rearmament programme being openly proclaimed. It was the same in 1936 when the Wehrmacht marched into the Rhineland which, under the Locarno Treaty, was to remain demilitarized; it was the same in March 1938 when Germany, not without a show of military force, accomplished the incorporation of Austria. In September that year she surrendered to Germany large territories of her ally Czechoslovakia in order to buy peace. A year later when – significantly six hours later than Britain – she finally declared war on Germany, more in sorrow than anger, because of Germany's attack on a second ally, Poland, she had stood by for three weeks. And during those three weeks but a single German army was facing the entire French armed forces while all the others were busy, far away in the east, finishing off Poland. Could such a country be capable of another Marne and another Verdun if attacked itself? Would it not collapse at the first blow, like Prussia in 1806, which, over eleven years, had similarly conducted a cowardly policy only to declare war at the very last and worst moment on a far superior Napoleon? Hitler was sure of his case. And, in fairness to him, he was right. The campaign in France was his greatest success.

However, what applies to all of Hitler's successes also applies to this. It was not the miracle that it appeared to the world to be. Whether he dealt the *coup de grâce* to the Weimar Republic or to the Paris peace system, whether he overran the German conservatives or France, Hitler invariably only toppled what was tottering and killed what was already dying. What he has to be credited with was an instinct for spotting what was already tottering and what was already dying and waiting merely to be put out of its agony. This instinct gave him an edge over all his rivals (he had had it even as a young man in the old Austria) and greatly impressed both his contemporaries and himself. But that instinct, undoubtedly a useful gift for a politician, had less in common with the eye of the eagle than with the nose of the vulture.

Misconceptions

T HE life of Man is short, the life of states and nations is long. Even social strata and classes, institutions and parties as a rule long survive the individuals who serve them as politicians. The result is that most politicians – and, interestingly enough, the more so the further to the Right they are – act purely pragmatically. They do not know the entire play in which they have their short scene, they cannot and do not even wish to know it; they merely act as the moment seems to bid them. By doing just that they are often more successful than those who pursue distant goals and, usually in vain, attempt to comprehend the meaning of the whole. There are even political agnostics (and these are often the most successful politicians) who do not believe that the whole has a meaning at all. To quote Bismarck, for example: 'What else are our states and their power and glory before God but ant-heaps and beehives which are crushed by the hoof of an ox or overtaken by destiny in the shape of a bee-keeper.'

The other type of politician, the one who tries to translate a theory into practice and, by serving his state or party, at the same time wishes to serve Providence, history or progress, is usually found on the Left wing, and he is as a rule less successful. Failed political idealists and Utopianists are as numerous as the sand of the sea. Nevertheless, a few great men have been successful even with this kind of politics, especially the great revolutionaries – Cromwell, for example, or Jefferson, and in our century Lenin and Mao. The fact that their success invariably looked different – uglier – from its expectation does not impair the success as such.

Hitler, and this is one of the main reasons why one should be very careful about placing him without further scrutiny on the political Right wing, very definitely belonged to that second kind of politician. He certainly did not wish to be merely a pragmatic politician but saw himself a political thinker and setter of goals, a 'programmatician', as he himself put it in a term existing only in his own vocabulary. In a sense he wanted to be not only the Lenin but also the Marx of Hitlerism, and he was particularly proud of the fact that in him the 'programmatician' and the politician were united in a way that happened, as he himself put it, 'only once within long periods of mankind'. Incidentally, he realized clearly that a politician working according to a theory, to a 'programme', as a rule had a harder task than the pure pragmatist: 'For the greater a man's work for the future, the more difficult is also his struggle and the rarer his success. If, nevertheless, it is given to but one in many centuries, then perhaps a soft glow of future glory may surround him in his latter days.'

That, as we know, was not given to Hitler. What surrounded him in his latter days was anything but the glow of future glory. But it is entirely correct that he made politics according to a home-made programme and that this complicated rather than facili-tated his politics. One could go as far as to say that he had virtually programmed his failure. The image of the world which he had made for himself and on which his programme was based happened to be incorrect. A policy aligned to that image could no more reach its goal than can a traveller using an incorrect map.

It is, therefore, worthwhile to take a closer look at Hitler's political concept of the world and to separate what was incorrect from what was correct or at least arguable. Strangely enough, this has scarcely been attempted so far. Prior to 1969, when Eberhard Jäckel produced a synthesis of 'Hitler's Ideology' from the dis-jointed mass of his ideas scattered among his books and speeches, the literature on Hitler even refused to acknowledge that any such ideology had existed. The prevailing opinion until then may be summed up in the words of Hitler's early English biographer Alan Bullock: 'The only principles of Nazism were power and rule for their own sake.' This point is made in specific contrast to, for instance, Robespierre and Lenin, for whom 'the will to power ... coincided with the triumph of a principle'. Hitler used to be regarded, and is still regarded by many who have failed to investigate the subject in depth, as a pure opportunist.

But he was anything but that. Much as he trusted his instinct, his 'intuition', in matters of tactics and timing, he based his poli-tical strategy very definitely upon firm and indeed rigid basic ideas which, moreover, he had so arranged for himself that they produced a reasonably logical system, if a little frayed at the edges – a 'theory' in the Marxist sense. In Jäckel's book this theory has been put together, posthumously as it were, from the many fragments and digressions in Hitler's political writings. But Jäckel has not gone beyond that point since he regarded a critique as superfluous: 'Among civilized people there is no need to argue the point that this ideology, whose means, undisguisedly and from the outset, were solely war and murder, has probably never been surpassed by any other in primitivity and brutality.' Only too true. It certainly is no pleasure to examine Hitler as a political thinker to the point that a critical analysis demands. Nevertheless it seems necessary to do so, and for two opposite reasons.

First, because until it has been done a greater portion of Hitler's theoretical ideas than one might think will survive, and not only among the Germans or among avowed followers of Hitler. Secondly, because until the misconceptions in these ideas are clearly separated from what was more or less correct in them, the correct elements are in danger of being made taboo simply because Hitler also thought so. But two and two still remain four even though Hitler would undoubtedly have agreed.

The latter danger is the greater because the starting points of Hitler's thinking were almost invariably unoriginal. The original element in them, which can be proved almost entirely to have been erroneous, is what he made of them. Just as, in his architectural designs, he started from the conventional neo-classical 'public buildings' style, against which there is little to be said, and subsequently ruined it by exaggerated, ostentatiously provocative proportions, so the basic ideas from which he proceeded in his political thinking were those which he shared with most of his contemporaries. Some of them indeed were such platitudes as 'two and two make four'.

One such platitude, for instance, is that there are different nations and also, though since Hitler's day one scarcely dares to use the word, different races. An almost universally accepted view in his day and one that still predominates today, was that states and nations should if possible coincide, in other words that states should be national states. Even the idea that wars cannot be ruled out from the life of states became questionable only after Hitler's day, while the question of how they are to be abolished has still not been answered. These are merely cautionary examples to show that what Hitler thought and said need not be rejected as beyond discussion merely because it was he who thought and said it. One should not, with the deadly name 'Hitler', shout down anyone who treats nations and races as the realities they are, or who supports the idea of the national state, or who faces the possibility of war. The fact that Hitler miscalculated does not abolish arithmetic.

Let us now try to present a brief outline of Hitler's historical-political ideology, the theory of 'Hitlerism'. It looks something like this.

The only actors in all historical processes are nations or races, not classes or religions, and strictly speaking not even states. History 'is the description of the course of a nation's struggle for its life'. Or, to pick another: 'Anything that happens in world history is merely the manifestation of the self-preservation of the races.' The state is 'in principle only a means to an end, and sees its end in the preservation of the racial existence of the people'. Or, a little less defensively: 'Its aim rests in the preservation *and promotion* of a community of physically and psychologically homogeneous human beings.' 'Domestic policy must ensure for a nation the inner strength to assert itself in its foreign policy.'

That foreign policy assertion consists in struggle: 'Whoever wants to live must therefore fight, and whoever does not wish to do battle in this world of eternal struggle does not deserve life', and struggle between nations (or races) normally and naturally takes the shape of war. Viewed correctly, 'wars lose the character of separate more or less massive surprises and take their place in a natural and comprehensible system of thorough-going well-founded lasting national development'.

Politics is the art of implementing a nation's vital struggle for its earthly existence. Foreign policy is the art of ensuring for a nation the amount and quality of living space it needs at a given time. Domestic policy is the art of procuring for a nation the power necessary for this, in the form of its racial quality and its numbers.

In short, politics is war and the preparation for war, and war is mainly about living space. That is universally valid, for all nations and even for all living creatures, because 'their instinct for self-preservation is infinite as is their longing for continued existence, whereas the space within which this entire life process unrolls is finite. In that limitation of living space lies the inevitability of existential struggle.' Specifically valid for the German nation is the point that 'it must rally its strength for its advance along that road which, from the nation's present confined living space, leads out to new land and soil'. Its main objective must be 'to remove the discrepancy between our population total and our territory – the latter viewed both as a source of nutrition and a power base'.

Secondly, however, wars are about domination and subjection. What the 'aristocratic basic idea of Nature desires is the victory of the strong and the annihilation of the weak or his unconditional subjection'. That is the essence of that 'free interplay of forces which must lead to a continuous improvement of the stock'.

Thirdly, however, and ultimately, the perpetual warlike struggle between nations is about world domination. This is expressed most clearly and most briefly in a speech of 13 November 1930: 'Every being strives for expansion and every nation strives for world domination.' And that is a good thing because 'we all feel that in the distant future man will find himself confronted by problems which only a supreme race, as a master nation based upon the resources and facilities of an entire globe, can be called upon to solve'. And right at the end of *Mein Kampf* we read, with unambiguous reference to Germany which must 'necessarily gain the position due to it on this earth': 'A state which, in an age of racial poisoning, devotes itself to the cultivation of its best racial elements must one day become master of the earth.'

So far the ideas are all a little narrow, steep and reckless but they have an inner logic. Things only begin to get confused when one observes Hitler juggling with the concept of the 'race', a key concept in Hitler's thinking ('the racial problem is the key to world history') but never defined by him and often equated with the concept of 'nation'. 'A supreme race as a master nation' shall, according to Hitler, rule the world one day – but which, a race or a nation? The Germans or the 'Aryans'? This is never entirely clear with Hitler. Equally unclear is whom he regards as an Aryan. Only the more or less Germanic nations? Or all Whites except the Jews? This is nowhere clarified by Hitler.

The concept of 'race' is applied, in general usage and also by Hitler, in two quite distinct senses, a value judgement sense and a neutral, descriptive one. 'Superior race', 'to improve the race' – these are value concepts from the sphere of the stockbreeder who, for each particular strain, will exclude inferior examples from breeding and try to improve certain racial characteristics by selective breeding. This is the sense in which Hitler often uses the term when he refers to the 'racial quality' of a nation, to be improved, for instance, by the sterilization of the feeble-minded or the killing of the mentally sick. The term 'race' is also applied, in general usage, as a neutral concept distinguishing different variants of the same species, and such variants, of course, exist among human beings as they do among horses or dogs. People of different colour are described, without any value judgement at all, as belonging to different races, and if, since Hitler, one has become reluctant to use that word then one will have to invent another word meaning the same thing. Moreover, to make the confusion worse, it had also been customary in Hitler's day to describe the various branches of the white race, i.e. ethnic groups such as the Germanic, Romance and Slav peoples, or the different types of physique or skull – Nordic, Eastern, Western or 'Dinaric' – as 'races', with a subsequent admixture of prejudices and arbitrary value judgements. 'Germanic' or 'Nordic' sounded more distinguished to many ears than 'Slavic' or 'Eastern'.

All this is in a complete muddle in Hitler's thinking, and Jäckel, whose praiseworthy account of Hitler's ideology we have so far substantially followed, possibly helps a little by trying to assign to Hitler's racial doctrine a firm and logically unassailable place in the general pattern. That is possible only if one leaves something out. Of course, so long as 'race' is used in the stock-breeding sense, as it sometimes is by Hitler, and one considers that a nation can or should improve its 'racial quality' by 'selective breeding', everything fits. The actors of history, in that case, are the nations, history itself consists of their wars, their rivalry for living space and world domination, and so for that struggle they must be perpetually rearmed; not only militarily and ideologically but also biologically, i.e. by raising their racial quality, by the elimination of the weak and by the deliberate selective breeding of their militarily useful characteristics. All that, of course, is nonsense – a point to which we shall return – but it is consistent within itself. But this is not the whole of Hitler's image of the world but only half of it. The other half is his anti-semitism, and to justify and rationalize that he needs the other meaning of 'race'. Indeed, one might say that he needs an entirely new theory, one that contradicts the former in several respects.

We have so far only once touched on Hitler's anti-semitism, in our outline of his biography when we observed that it was the first thing that took root in him, even before his Greater-German nationalism. From now onwards we shall have to deal with it, to our disgust, in every chapter. His assessment of the Jews was not only the most fateful of his misconceptions but his Jewish policy was also the first mistake he made in his practical politics; his gravest crime was committed against the Jews and in the betrayal which Hitler finally committed against Germany his anti-semitic obsession played a considerable part. At this point we shall only concern ourselves with the misconceptions in his anti-semitic theory.

This is again an entire theory of its own and would require very elaborate manipulation to make it harmonize with his first theory, which one might call his ethnic theory. According to the former all history consists of the continuous struggle of nations for living space. Now we are suddenly informed that this is not the whole of history after all. Alongside the struggle of nations there is, according to Hitler, yet another permanent feature of history – the racial struggle, by which he means not a struggle between white and black and yellow-skinned people (the real racial differences between white, black and yellow-skinned people did not interest Hitler at all), but a struggle within the white race, namely between the 'Aryans' and the Jews. In other words, between the Jews and all the rest, who might otherwise be in continuous struggle against each other but who, against the Jews, all belong to the same side. This struggle is not about living space, but literally about life; it is a struggle of extermination. 'The Jew' is everybody's enemy: 'His ultimate aim is the de-nationalization, the inter-bastardization of the other nations, the lowering of the racial level of the noblest, as well as domination over that racial jumble through the extermination of the national intelligentsias and their replacement by members of his own nation.' And more than that: 'If the Jew with the aid of his Marxist creed remains victorious over the nations of this world, then his crown will be the wreath on the grave of mankind, then this planet will once more, as millions of years ago, move through the ether devoid of human beings.' The Jews apparently intend to exterminate not only the 'national intelligentsias' but the whole of mankind. If that is so then of course the whole of mankind must unite to exterminate them in their turn, and in this capacity as exterminator of the Jews Hitler presents himself not as a specifically German politician but as the champion of the whole of mankind: 'By fighting off the Jew I fight for the work of the Lord.' In his political testament he calls 'international Jewry' the 'world-wide poisoner of all nations', and his final dictation to Bormann of 2 April 1945 concludes with the words: 'People will be eternally grateful to National Socialism that I have extinguished the Jews in Germany and Central Europe.' Here he positively presents himself as an internationalist and a benefactor of humanity.

We are not at this point criticizing Hitler's thought (difficult though it is to present this homicidal nonsense uncritically) – we are presenting it. But even a mere presentation demands an answer to three questions.

First, what were the Jews in Hitler's eyes? A religion, a nation, or a race?

Second, what, according to Hitler, were they doing that made them so dangerous to all other nations that they should deserve such a terrible fate?

Third, how was Hitler's doctrine of the perpetual struggle between the Jews and everybody else compatible with his doctrine of the (equally perpetual and equally God-given) struggle of everybody else against everybody else?

Hitler certainly tried to find answers to these three questions but all the answers come out somewhat confused and artificial; here are the frayed margins of Hitler's world of ideas.

On the first question only one thing was clear to Hitler – that the Jews were not a religious community. This he repeated indefatigably without ever justifying it, although surely it would need justification. After all it is evident that there is such a thing as a Jewish religion and that it was this religion which held the Jews together as Jews throughout nearly 1,900 years of the Diaspora. However, to Hitler they were not a religious community. Whether they were a race or a nation Hitler evidently never quite decided in his own mind. True, he kept referring to the Jewish race, moreover in the dual sense of 'distinct race' and also 'inferior race'; but in his second book, which contains the most careful elaboration of his theory of anti-semitism, he calls them, probably more accurately, a nation, and even concedes to them what he concedes to other nations: 'Just as any nation possesses, as the basic tendency underlying its entire earthly activity, the longing to preserve itself as a living force, so this is true also of Jewry.' But he immediately adds: 'However, in line with the fundamentally different character of the Aryan nations and of Jewry, their existential struggle is also different in its forms.'

The Jews – and here we come to Hitler's answer to the second question – were by their very nature international, incapable of establishing a state. 'Jewish' and 'international' were virtually synonymous to Hitler; anything that was international was Jewish, and in this context Hitler even spoke of a Jewish state: 'The Jewish State has never been limited territorially but has been universal and unlimited in extent; it is, however, confined to one race.' And therefore – here we have it – this 'Jewish state' was 'international world Jewry', the enemy of all other states, against which it was mercilessly fighting with all means at its disposal, in external politics by pacifism and internationalism, capitalism and communism, in domestic politics by parliamentarianism and democracy. All these were tools for the weakening and destruction of the state, all were inventions of the Jews and all aimed at only one thing – to disrupt and weaken the 'Aryan' nations in their magnificent struggle for living space (a struggle in which the Jews, cunningly, did not participate) in order thus to ensure their own pernicious world domination.

And this brings us to Hitler's answer to the third question. Why did all nations have to unite against the Jews when surely they had their hands full fighting against each other for living space? Answer: they had to unite just *because* they had to fight for their living space, and *in order that* they might devote themselves undisturbed to their pre-ordained struggle. The Jews were the spoilsports in this pleasant game; with their internationalism and pacifism, their (international) capitalism and their (equally international) communism they were diverting the 'Aryan' nations from their main task and their main occupation, and that is why they had to be removed from the world, and not from Germany only. Moreover they had to be removed not like a piece of furniture that is taken away to be put elsewhere, but like a stain that is removed by wiping it out. Nor must they be left with an escape.

If they abandoned their religion that meant nothing since they were not a religious community but a race, and if they tried to escape even their race by intermingling with 'Aryans', then that was worse still because they thereby impaired the 'Aryan' race and rendered the nation concerned incapable of its necessary existential struggle. And if they tried to integrate with that nation and become German, French, English or other patriots, then that was the worst thing of all, for their aim would then be 'to push the nations into wars against each other [but surely this was just what, according to Hitler, the nations were for?] and in that way gradually, with the help of the power of money and propaganda, raise themselves to being masters over them'. Quite obviously, whatever the Jews did they were always wrong, and in any case they had to be exterminated.

That, then, is Hitler's second, anti-semitic, theory, which stands independently alongside the ethnic one and cannot readily be harmonized with it. The two together make up what may be called 'Hitlerism', the ideological edifice of Hitler the 'programmatician' – his counterpart, in a sense, to Marxism.

Hitlerism has at least one thing in common with Marxism – the claim to be able to explain the whole of world history from one single point of view. 'The history of all society so far is a history of class struggles', we read in the Communist Manifesto, and analogously in Hitler, 'All events in world history are merely the manifestation of the self-preservation drive of the races'. Such sentences have considerable emotive power. Anyone reading them has the feeling of suddenly seeing the light; what had been confused becomes simple, what had been difficult becomes easy. To those who willingly accept them such statements give an agreeable sense of enlightenment and knowledge, and they moreover arouse a certain furious impatience with those who do *not* accept them, since in all such words of command there is a ring of '... and anything else is a lie'. This mixture of swaggering superiority and intolerance is found equally among convinced Marxists and convinced Hitlerites.

It is, of course, an error that 'all history' is either this or that. History is a jungle, and no clearing that one cuts into it opens up the whole forest. History has known class struggles *and* racial clashes, and also conflicts (indeed more frequently) between states, nations, faiths, ideologies, and so on. There is no conceivable human community that might not, in certain circumstances, find itself in conflict with another – and, historically, it is hard to find one which has not at some time been so.

But history – and that is the second error in such dictatorial statements – does not consist solely of fighting. Both nations and classes have lived over much longer periods in peace with one another than at war, and the means by which they achieve this peace are at least as interesting and worthy of historical research as are the factors which, from time to time, lead them into warlike clashes.

One of those means is the state, and it is significant that in Hitler's political system the state plays an entirely subordinate part. Once before, in a totally different context, when we were considering Hitler's achievements, we came up against the astonishing fact that he was no statesman, indeed that he had made every effort long before the war to destroy whatever remnants of German state structure he inherited, and that he replaced it by a chaos of 'states within the state'. Now, in Hitler's ideology, we find the theoretical justification for this blunder. Hitler was not interested in the state, did not understand the state, and actually did not think much of it. He was concerned only with nations and races, not with states. The state to him was 'only a means to an end', the end, in brief, being the waging of war. Consequently Hitler did not omit anything during the years 1933–39 with regard to war preparations, but what he created was a war machine not a state. And for that he had to pay dearly.

A state is not only a war machine – at most, it may *possess* one – nor is it necessarily the political organization of a nation. The idea of the national state is no older than two hundred years. Most states in history comprised, or still comprise, many nations, such as the great empires of antiquity, or indeed the present-day Soviet

Union; or else they comprised only portions of a nation, such as the city states of antiquity and the present-day German states. For all that they do not cease to be states, nor do they cease to be necessary. The idea of the state is much older than the national idea; and states do not exist principally for the purpose of waging wars, but, on the contrary, for the preservation and safeguarding of the external and domestic peace of their inhabitants, no matter whether these are nationally homogeneous or not. States are systems of order. War, no less than civil war, is for them an exceptional emergency; in order to cope with such emergencies, states have their monopoly of power, their armed forces and their police, but they do not have it in order to conquer living space for one nation at the expense of other nations, or for waging wars to improve the race, or to attain world domination.

None of this was known to Hitler – or perhaps one should say: he did not want to know about it. For there is no denying the voluntarist trait in Hitler's view of the world: he saw the world as he *wanted* to see it. That the world is imperfect, full of conflict, hardship and suffering, including the world of states which is riddled with mistrust, fear and war – this is only too true, and it is quite right not to shut one's eyes to it. So long as he says no more than that, Hitler stands firmly on the ground of truth. Except that he does not state these things with the sad courageous earnestness with which Luther calmly faced what he called original sin, or Bismarck what he called earthly imperfection, but with that frenzied voice with which Nietzsche, for instance, so often hailed what was deplorable. To Hitler the emergency was the norm, the state was there in order to wage war. And that is where he was wrong. The world is not like that, not even the world of states. In the world of states, such as it is, wars are invariably waged for peace; and not only defensive wars but also aggressive wars if they have any meaning at all. Every war ends with a peace treaty or a state treaty and, hence, with a new state of peace which as a rule persists much longer than the state of war which preceded it. Once the military decision has taken place peace must be concluded, or else the war would have been pointless. The fact that

Hitler failed to see that – did not wish to see it – resulted, as we shall see in the next chapter, in one of his most disastrous mistakes.

In Hitler's view of the world, moreover, wars always were wars of conquest with the aim of gaining living space for the warring nation, of permanently subjecting (or annihilating) the vanquished, and ultimately achieving world domination. This was another misconception on his part. Wars for the sake of living space had not been waged in Europe, prior to Hitler, since the Migration of the Peoples, that is for roughly one and a half millenia. Europe was settled; its nations were firmly located; and if, as the result of a peace treaty, some province or other changed hands from one state to another, or even if an entire state, as for example Poland, was partitioned among its neighbours, the inhabitants remained where they were. Living space was neither won nor lost: living space was not fought over in Europe. Only Hitler, after an interval of roughly 1,500 years, reintroduced this feature into European history, with terrible consequences for Germany. Expulsion, such as that of the Germans from their former eastern territories, was precisely what Hitler had always preached as the purpose of any war and what he himself had put into practice in conquered Poland.

'Living space' was a misconception also for another reason. The point is that in the twentieth century it no longer pays to fight for living space. If Hitler measured a nation's prosperity and power by the extent of the territory inhabited and farmed by it, if he demanded and pursued a 'territorial policy', then he overlooked, or deliberately ignored, the industrial revolution. Since the industrial revolution prosperity and power have no longer depended on the size of one's territory but on the state of one's technology. And for that, the size of one's living space is irrelevant.

Indeed an excess of 'living space,' that is great territorial expanse with sparse population, can be a positive handicap for a country's technological-industrial development – a fact well known, for instance, to the Soviet Union: it simply cannot manage to open up and develop Siberia, a vast territory rich in raw materials, but too sparsely populated. It is certainly an unmistakable fact that some of the poorest and weakest countries in today's world are enormous, while some of the richest and most secure are minute. Hitler, who certainly was a modern thinker in some areas – such as military technology or the motorization of the masses – was totally and entirely rooted in the pre-industrial age with his living-space theory.

But just that misconception of Hitler's refuses to lie down. Nostalgia for the pre-industrial age and an anxious malaise with the 'inhuman' man-made world we have been bringing upon ourselves ever more rapidly for the past two hundred years, were not only widespread in Hitler's day but are again particularly strong at present. They made Hitler's living-space ideas seem sensible to many of his contemporaries – did not Germany really look much too small on the map in relation to her strength and population total? True, if Germany were to become a predominantly peasant country again – on this point Hitler's thinking agreed strangely with Morgenthau's – then she really did need more living space. But only then.

The idea that the wars of the twentieth century were ultimately about world domination is also older than Hitler and has survived him. Even before the First World War Kurt Riezler, the adviser of Reich Chancellor Bethmann-Hollweg, a highly educated man, wrote: 'In its ideas . . . every nation strives to grow, to spread itself, to dominate and subjugate without end; it strives to unite itself ever more firmly and to incorporate ever new elements into itself, to become an organic unit under its rule.' That is pure Hitler, except that the language is more unctuous. But it was nevertheless wrong; not every nation has those aims. Or are the Swiss and the Swedes not nations? Not even the European great powers during the period of European colonial imperialism can be said, each of them for itself, to have aspired to world domination. They had learned the lesson too well, over the centuries, that they could not abolish one another and that any attempt to attain hegemony even in Europe would inevitably bring about a coalition of the remaining great powers, who would feel threatened and combine to foil any such attempt.

Even the Pan-Germans of the Kaiser's Germany in their dreams of German world power meant as a rule no more than that Germany as a 'world power' should be ranged alongside the others. They were thinking of a great German colonial empire in Asia and Africa, supported by German predominance on the European continent – not of world conquest or world rule in the literal meaning.

Hitler, on the other hand, clearly meant it quite literally when he spoke of world rule, even though he scarcely expected to achieve more in his own lifetime than German rule over the whole of Europe including, in particular, Russia (he was not greatly interested in colonies). The 'Greater Germanic Reich', into which he intended to transform conquered Europe and in which the nations were to be melted in a new racial hierarchy, was then to become the springboard towards real world domination.

There is, of course, some truth in the argument that our world, shrunk through technology and threatened by weapons of mass destruction, is calling out for unity and that, therefore, the idea of world rule – world unity, world government, world rule, all these lie close together – has become topical again in the twentieth century. Hitler's misconception was not in taking the idea of world rule up. It was in seeing the German Reich as a serious candidate for world domination. The Germany of his day undoubtedly was a great power, in fact the strongest in Europe, but still only one among several, and one that had failed once before in the attempt to become both the leading power in Europe and a world power. Only if the union of Europe had been accomplished – and that was not to be achieved by wars of conquest and subjugation – might such a united Europe, in which Germany would then have to be absorbed, have had a chance in rivalry for world rule. But the unification of Europe – surely that would have been Jewish internationalism! Hitler instead believed that he was able to achieve his goal with a national Greater Germany alone, by racial policy and anti-semitism – a primitive misconception. A biological rearmament of Germany by racial improvement in the stockbreeding sense would have required several generations, quite apart from all the problems involved; and Hitler wanted to achieve everything he intended in his own lifetime. As for anti-semitism, Hitler was wrong not only about the Jews but even about the anti-semites.

Hitler really believed – this is proved not only by his quoted written and public statements but also by oral and private remarks made during the war – that his anti-semitism would gain him world-wide sympathy for the German cause, that it would make Germany's cause the cause of mankind. He counted on the existence of anti-semites throughout the world. But Hitler's variety of anti-semitism, demanding extermination, existed nowhere except in eastern Europe, from where he himself had got it; and even there, it must be said to the credit of the Ukrainians, Poles and Lithuanians, it was based not on Hitler's fantasies of a world-wide Jewish conspiracy to enslave or exterminate 'Aryan' humanity, but upon the plain fact that the Jews in those countries were settled as a compact alien people. This was not the case anywhere else, and accordingly anti-semitism elsewhere never aimed at the extermination or the 'removal' of the Jews.

For the most part, where it did exist, it was of a religious character: after all, until the Second Vatican Council, the Catholic Church in particular had been in open conflict with the Jews as unbelievers. The aim of that religious anti-semitism, by far the most widespread kind, was not the extermination of the Jews but their conversion; the moment they were baptized all was well.

There was also a social anti-semitism, especially in rural areas. There the Jews were hated as money-lenders – often, as is well known, the only occupation they were allowed to practise prior to their emancipation. That social anti-semitism, paradoxically as it may sound, aimed at the emancipation of the Jews. As soon as Jews appeared in functions other than that of money-lender that type of anti-semitism disappeared: Jewish doctors, for instance, where they existed, were invariably highly esteemed and much in demand.

Finally, there was a new, post-emancipation anti-semitism which might be called competition anti-semitism. Since their emancipation, that is roughly since the mid-nineteenth century, the Jews, partly through their talent and partly also, as has to be admitted, by sticking together, had reached leading positions in various fields in many countries – especially in all fields of culture, but also in medicine, the law, the press, industry, finance, science and politics. They proved to be if not exactly the salt of the earth then certainly, in many countries, the salt in the soup: they formed a kind of élite. In the Weimar Republic, at least in Berlin under the Weimar Republic, they even formed something like a second aristocracy. That, needless to say, earned them not only deserved admiration but also envy and dislike. Anyone who was an anti-semite on those grounds was pleased to see the Jews getting a knock now and again. But extermination – for God's sake! What Hitler's specific kind of homicidal Jew-phobia and Jew-hatred produced even among anti-semites in other countries was initially, so long as he raged only verbally, a shaking of heads; and subsequently, when he proceeded to act, frequently real horror. The run-of-the-mill anti-semites shared few of the misconceptions and fallacies spread by Hitler about the Jews. We shall now briefly examine these – briefly, because for the most part they refute themselves by their mere presentation.

No matter how often Hitler asserted that the Jews were not a religious community, anyone could see that the opposite was true. The Jewish religion stands as a huge rock before the eyes of the world: the first and still the purest monotheistic religion, the only one that has dared to think out, undiluted and unsoftened, the enormous idea of the One nameless, imageless, incomprehensible and unfathomable God, and has persisted in it; and probably the only one that was able, through nineteen centuries of the Diaspora and intermittent persecution, to hold its believers together as a community of faith. Hitler did not see that, he probably quite genuinely was blind to it. He was, in spite of his customary rhetorical appeals to 'Providence' and the 'Almighty', not only ir-religious himself but also had no perception of what religion can mean to others. His handling of the Christian Churches clearly revealed that.

On the other hand, the Jews quite patently are not a race – not even if one is prepared to apply the concept of 'race' to the various tribes and variants of the white race. Present-day Israel, for example, is a clearly multi-racial state, as any visitor can discover with his own eyes; and the reason is that Judaism has always been a missionary, proselytizing religion. Members of all nations, tribes and variants of the white race in the Roman Empire became Jews in late Roman days, though not perhaps quite as many as became Christians at the time; for several centuries Judaism and Christianity were in missionary competition with each other. There are even some Jews, though not many, who belong to the black or the yellow races. And Arthur Koestler has recently made out a credible case to the effect that the eastern Jews, in particular, those who suffered worst under Hitler, were most of them probably not Semites at all but descendants of the Khazars, a Turkic people originally settled between the Volga and the Caucasus, who adopted the Jewish religion in the Middle Ages and subsequently migrated towards the west and north-west. (To that extent even the word 'anti-semitism' is inaccurate but, since it has become the current term, we are using it here.)

Can the Jews be called a people, a nation? That is more debatable. Without any doubt they lack what identifies nations most clearly – a common language. English Jews speak English, French Jews French, German Jews German, etc. It is also true that many – probably most – Jews have, since their civil emancipation, become good patriots of their respective home countries, at times, and especially in Germany, super-patriots. Nevertheless, a certain Jewish sense of belonging together, a solidarity across national frontiers, a Jewish sense of nationhood, has lately become particularly marked in the shape of a general Jewish solidarity with Israel. And that is hardly surprising: religion often serves nations which have not had a state of their own for a long period as a national cement. Thus, the Catholicism of the Poles and the Irish has, in addition to its religious component, unmistakable nationalist ingredients. Among the Jews, who had lived without a state of their own very much longer than the Poles or the Irish, this national tie and nation-building force of religion has possibly been even stronger. Frequent persecution further served to make the Jews stick together. Something of this binding force of religion (and persecution) is active probably even among those who, as individuals, have abandoned their faith. The same may be observed among the members of other religions. A lapsed Protestant and a lapsed Catholic differ no less in their way of thinking than a Protestant does from a Catholic. Their mental habits remain impregnated by the religion of their fathers and forefathers, often for several generations. With a religion as strong as Judaism it may take even longer for the effects to evaporate among the apostates.

None of that is a reason for being an anti-semite, let alone for persecuting the Jews with that murderous hatred and wish to exterminate them by Hitler evinced from the very beginning. That specifically Hitlerian hatred of the Jews can only be diagnosed as a clinical phenomenon, especially as Hitler's justification of it is so clearly retrospective. The existence of a world-wide Jewish conspiracy to exterminate all 'Aryans' is patently not just a misconception but paranoid nonsense. Or perhaps not even that but the ingenious rationalization of a preconceived resolution to do murder. At all events, it is incorrect in all respects. 'World Jewry' not only did not pursue the sinister aims which Hitler fancifully attributed to it; it had no common aims of any kind. On the contrary, especially in Hitler's day, it was more disunited and often more divided in its attitudes than it had ever been before in its 3,000 years of history: between traditional religiosity and modern secularization, between assimilation and Zionism, between nationalism and internationalism. Furthermore, all the major divisions of the world also ran right through Jewry which, since the civil emancipation of the Jews, had been integrated with the world in a manner unknown before. Many Jews had indeed been busy, for a century or half a century, deliberately abandoning their identity through assimilation, conversion and intermarriage, and being wholly absorbed in their respective native countries; and nowhere was that process taking place with so much conviction and fervour as in Germany. Naturally, there was also among many Jews stubborn resistance to that trend. In short, the Jews, whom Hitler pretended to see as a community of conspirators as powerful as they were diabolical, were in fact a community in deep crisis, weakened as never before, often in a state of incipient dissolution, when his frightful attack fell upon them. They went as lambs to the slaughter, and the would-be slayer of dragons was murdering the helpless.

Mistakes

AN examination of the mistakes committed by Hitler runs into two obstacles. The first is the same as that already encountered in our consideration of Hitler's misconceptions: the inclination, from the very start and without examination, to describe anything that Hitler thought as a misconception merely because it was Hitler who thought so is paralleled by an inclination to condemn as a mistake anything Hitler did from start to finish, merely because it was Hitler who did it. A very understandable prejudice but not, of course, conducive to real understanding or sound judgement.

The other obstacle lies in the tendency, predominating in present-day historical research, to make historiography come as close as possible to an exact science, i.e. to search for regular patterns, to focus attention mainly on social and economic development where such regularities may be presumed to be more probable, to play down, in consequence, the role of the political elements proper in history and, most particularly, to deny the influence of policy-making individuals, the effects of 'great men' on the course of history. Hitler, of course, does not fit into that trend, and any supporter of it is bound to regard it as a downright presumption to expect a serious historian to examine the question of what a single individual, who was on the political stage for only fifteen years, had done right or done wrong, and even possibly to trace it to his individual character traits, especially when one is dealing with so unattractive a character as Hitler. Surely all that is old hat!

However, one may feel on the contrary that a phenomenon such as Hitler proves that this entire historical trend is on the wrong track. The same applies to the phenomena of Lenin and Mao, whose immediate effect, however, was confined to their own countries whereas Hitler pushed the whole world into a new direction – though admittedly a different direction from the one he had intended. Just that makes his case so complex and so interesting.

It is impossible for a serious historian to maintain that without Hitler world history in the twentieth century would have taken the course it has taken. It is by no means certain that without Hitler a second world war would even have taken place; it is quite certain that *if* it had taken place it would have taken a different course – possibly even with entirely different alliances, fronts and outcomes. Today's world, whether we like it or not, is the work of Hitler. Without Hitler there would have been no partition of Germany and Europe; without Hitler there would be no Americans and no Russians in Berlin; without Hitler there would be no Israel; without Hitler there would be no de-colonialization, at least not such a rapid one; there would be no Asian, Arab or Black African emancipation, and no diminution of European pre-eminence. Or, more accurately, there would be none of all this without Hitler's mistakes. He certainly did not want any of it.

One has to go back a long way in history – perhaps to Alexander the Great – to find a man who, in a below-average short span of life, transformed the world so fundamentally and lastingly as Hitler. But what one would not find in the whole of world history is a man who, with an unparalleled and gigantic effort, achieved, as Hitler did, the exact opposite of what he had hoped to achieve.

What Hitler had hoped to achieve was Germany's hegemony in Europe and direct rule over Russia; elsewhere preservation of European rule over Africa and large parts of Asia and Oceania. A power pyramid, with the old European overseas colonies and the new German colony of Russia at its base, with the other European countries, graduated into Germany's ancillary countries, auxiliary nations, satellites, pseudo-independent or semi-independent allies at middle level, and Germany at the apex. This huge German-dominated power structure was to have been capable, at a later date, of taking on America and Japan in a struggle for world domination, and of doing so with good prospects of success.

What Hitler has achieved is the hegemony of America in Western and of Russia in Eastern Europe, accompanied by the

Mistakes

partition of Germany, and the dissolution of all European colonial empires. A world with two power peaks, in which the former European colonies are suddenly enjoying independence and a certain fool's licence, while Europe (again with certain graduations) is subordinated to the two super powers. In this pattern Germany, having totally lost her state structure, was at first right at the bottom and has taken years and decades to work her way up again, divided and occupied, to that status of dependent alliance with America and Russia, respectively, in which the rest of Europe is locked.

In other words: Hitler achieved the opposite of what he aimed at. Like no other 'great man' in recorded history he missed his mark with a giant's blow. The tremendous effect which he has produced, however, is beyond dispute, as is also the fact that twice – in the autumn of 1938 and in the summer of 1940 – he came very close to his real goal. It is therefore no idle game but an entirely serious historical exercise to identify the mistakes which caused him to convert what he had half-achieved into its opposite, and it is not just morbid curiosity if, in doing so, one concerns oneself also with Hitler's character. Most of his mistakes had their roots in his faults.

Partly, of course, also in his misconceptions. At least *one* mistake – the very first, which began to show even in 1933 – had been mapped out by Hitler the 'programmatician' for Hitler the politician.

In the preceding chapter we have seen that two totally different lines of action ran alongside one another in Hitler's theory of world events. On the one hand there was the perpetual struggle of the nations – more accurately the white nations; the coloured ones did not count for Hitler – for living space and domination or subjection, with world domination by one nation as the highest prize for the victor; on the other hand there was a joint struggle of all white nations against the Jews. Accordingly, Hitler the politician pursued two totally different aims from the very outset: Germany's rule over Europe on the one hand, and the 'removal' of the Jews, meaning their extermination, on the other. Neither had anything to do with the other; the two objectives actually obstructed each other.

It is always a mistake in politics to pursue two aims simultaneously – the more so if even the first aim is so ambitious that it can at best be attained by the utmost concentration of all strength and then only with a lot of luck. Everyone so far who had set himself the goal of dominating Europe had foundered – Charles v and Philip ii as much as Louis xiv and Napoleon. This was not perhaps necessarily a reason for dismissing any new attempt as hopeless from the start: it was at least conceivable that Germany in the twentieth century might succeed where Spain in the sixteenth and France in the seventeenth and nineteenth had failed. But it *was* a reason for not needlessly increasing the enormous predictable obstacles to the project by the addition of one that had nothing to do with the matter. Anyone wishing to conquer Europe ought not to have added to the number of enemies who would predictably arise in Europe by making scattered but influential enemies throughout the world (and in his own country). That was a mistake, especially when those arbitrarily made, additional enemies had previously been best friends. And that is what the Jews were until Hitler turned them into enemies.

It makes little difference how high one assesses the influence of the Jews on the politics of their respective countries. Hitler probably overestimated it – which should have been one more reason for keeping them on his side and not needlessly pushing them into the enemy camp. Prior to Hitler Jewish influence in the world had predominantly been a pro-German element, a fact which Germany's opponents in the First World War were only too well aware of. In America it had long and effectively opposed the country's entry into the war on the side of the Entente. In Russia it had played an important part in the revolution, successfully operated from Germany, against the Tsarist Empire. By his anti-semitism Hitler not only needlessly created additional enemies throughout the world, he also made enemies of friends, and he transferred a weight which had previously been on the German side of the balance over to the other side – a double loss.

Mistakes

The handicap which Hitler saddled himself with from the very outset by his anti-semitism in Germany itself is also under-estimated, even though that anti-semitism initially manifested itself only in continuous humiliation, defamation and discrimination of the German Jews and did not at once reveal its horrific final forms. Humiliation is quite sufficient to turn friends into enemies. And the German Jews in their great majority were positively in love with Germany right until Hitler – a small number, touchingly, still is, even after Hitler and in spite of Hitler.

The Jews had become good patriots in all Western countries since their emancipation. But nowhere had that Jewish patriotism such fervent, deeply emotional features as in Germany. One might speak of a Jewish love affair with Germany during the half century prior to Hitler (in his book *Doppelgänger, du bleicher Geselle*, Jorg von Uthmann has made a first attempt to get to the bottom of this specific Jewish–German affinity). And there is no doubt that the Jews were the lovers; the Germans at best, flattered and slightly bewildered, allowed themselves to be idolized by their Jewish fellow countrymen – unless they rejected it as Jewish importunity. Certainly this Jewish–German love affair produced some wonderful flowers in the cultural field; one need think only of the publisher Samuel Fischer and his authors, or of Max Reinhardt and his actors. There is no doubt that German Jews played an outstanding part, during the first third of the twentieth century, in helping Germany – for the first time – to outstrip Britain and France in the intellectual and cultural sphere as well as in science and economic life.

That came to a sudden end in 1933. Hitler saw to it that among most German Jews their humiliated love turned to hatred; and in addition to the German Jews he made enemies also of those Germans – admittedly not the majority but certainly not the worst Germans – who remained loyal to their Jewish friends. What passive resistance there was to the wave of Hitlerism in Germany was mainly caused by his anti-semitism.

The extent to which this silent non-participation of a not quite negligible minority weakened Hitler cannot, of course, be assessed.

The fact, for instance, that almost everyone of any standing in German literature went into exile was something that did not bother Hitler much. It was nevertheless an imponderable contribution to Hitler Germany's reputation in the world being ruined from the start. More serious was the blood-letting which Hitler's anti-semitism caused to German science. Not just the Jewish scientists, with Einstein at their head, emigrated. Important non-Jewish scientists followed their Jewish colleagues or teachers, and the foreign scientists who used to come to Germany in large numbers in the past now stayed away. Until Hitler the world centre of nuclear research had been Göttingen; in 1933 it shifted to America. It is an interesting speculation that, but for Hitler's anti-semitism, Germany and not America might have been the first power to develop an atom bomb.

Handicapping himself with anti-semitism was without doubt Hitler's first serious mistake, a mistake that is still being underestimated. Of course, other mistakes had to be added for the measure to overflow.

For in spite of the damage which Hitler's anti-semitism did to the German cause from the outset, the fact remains that twice Hitler came very close to his goal – in the autumn of 1938, when, with the full agreement of Britain and France, he was conceded a position of hegemony in Eastern Europe, and in the summer of 1940, when his victory over France and the occupation of many other countries laid almost the whole continent this side of Russia at his feet. This raises the question of whether German domination or hegemony in or over Europe was in itself a Utopian aim, i.e. whether that aim of Hitler's was likewise a mistake from the very start. Nowadays, if it is asked at all, the question is generally answered in the affirmative without much debate, even in the Federal Republic, and especially by the younger generation who often stare at their fathers and grandfathers as though they were lunatics ever to have set themselves such a goal. However, it should be remembered that the majority of those fathers and grandfathers, i.e. the generation of the First and that of the

Second World War, regarded that goal as reasonable and attainable. They were inspired by it and not infrequently died for it.

Naturally, this does not prove that the goal was attainable or desirable. Few, in fact, would today say that it was. But if one recalls the situation of Europe in the autumn of 1938 or in the summer of 1940 and keeps it in view long enough for a thorough inspection, and even more if one compares the sorry state of post-Hitler Europe with the position that pre-Hitler Europe held in the world, surely one begins to wonder. If Europe had wanted to maintain that position in the world, was it not really dependent on unification? Could that unification have been accomplished without forcible persuasion, and did it not require, at least at the initial stage, the hegemony of its strongest power? And was that strongest power not Germany? It was not only Germans – two generations of Germans – who answered such questions in the affirmative. The years 1938 and 1940 showed that a great many non-German Europeans also, though possibly with some reservations, were prepared to utter a hesitant 'yes'. And what happened after 1945 showed that quite conceivably they might not even have been entirely wrong, or, to put it another way, would not have been wrong provided the Germany they were dealing with had not been Hitler's Germany.

A Europe dominated by Hitler would undoubtedly have been a nightmare, just as Germany dominated by Hitler was a nightmare in many respects, with its persecution of the Jews and its concentration camps, its constitutional chaos, its lawlessness and enforced cultural provinciality. All this apart, one should not forget that the nineteenth-century European balance of power was no longer to be saved in the twentieth. The First World War and the peace which followed it had destroyed its core, and Britain's and France's half-hearted and hesitant attempt to restore it in 1939 had failed by 1940. The test of the Second World War has proved that Europe in the twentieth century only had the choice between German and American–Russian hegemony. Let there be no doubt: given the nature of a German hegemony under Hitler, an American one was far preferable and even a Russian one slightly so, although some people would dispute the latter. On the other hand, a German hegemony would have united Europe, whereas an American–Russian one must inevitably have divided it. A Europe united under German hegemony might have preserved its imperial hegemony in Asia and Africa for quite a while, but a Europe divided between America and Russia was bound to lose it precipitately.

That makes it understandable why, in Eastern Europe in 1938 and throughout the entire continent in 1940, following his victory over France, Hitler encountered a certain readiness for arrangement and submission. Certainly there did not then exist any European longing for unification comparable in strength, for instance, to the German longing for unification about the middle of the nineteenth century. That only emerged after 1945, when it was too late. But a readiness to yield to force and to make the best of submission to superior force was certainly present even in 1938 and 1940, and, at least sporadically, it was linked with a dim realization that Europe could perhaps do with a higher measure of unity, even at the cost of (possibly only initial) German hegemony. Memories were still alive of how Bismarck's Prussia had united the defeated German states in 1866 – and had itself subsequently been gradually absorbed into the Germany thus unified. Was it not conceivable that a victorious Germany would be similarly absorbed in a unified Europe and in the process gradually lose its repulsive features? And might not this desirable process be accelerated by complacency? Such reflections were widespread in 1940 in nearly all countries of Europe, especially in France, even though nobody wants to remember them today.

Whatever the sociological school of historiography might say, it depended on Hitler whether there would emerge a unified and strengthened (if initially German-dominated) Europe from that situation or what in fact has emerged from it. 'I was Europe's last chance', Hitler dictated to Bormann in February 1945 – and in a certain sense he was right.

Except that he should have added: 'And I wrecked it.'

Mistakes

Wrecking Europe was his second big mistake – after the first one of encumbering his German European policy with his anti-semitism. To understand how and why he wrecked it – and not once but twice – we must take a closer look at his policy in the autumn of 1938 and in the summer of 1940. It emerges that he either twice failed to see the chances that offered themselves to him, or that he deliberately threw them away – a double error as serious as the more conspicuous mistakes of 1941, when he attacked Russia and declared war on America.

First a brief run-down of the facts.

In March 1938 Hitler, by the *Anschluss* of Austria, had turned the German Reich into the Greater German Reich, and in September of the same year Britain and France, in the Munich Agreement, granted to that Greater German Reich the further incorporation of the German-settled border regions of Bohemia and Moravia. The Munich Agreement meant far more than merely the dismemberment of Czechoslovakia, which had relied in vain on its alliance with France. It virtually meant Britain's and France's political withdrawal from the Eastern half of Europe and the recognition of Eastern Europe right up to the Russian frontier as a German sphere of influence. The truncated Czechoslovak state left after the Munich Agreement was henceforth as wax in Hitler's hand. Poland and Hungary, whom he allowed to participate in the rape of Czechoslovakia, had thereby become his allies – the weak allies of a strong partner. Romania and Yugoslavia, already economically so closely linked with Germany that one could speak of dependence, now had to seek the closest political ties with her as well, since their French alliance had been made worthless by Munich. Bulgaria and Turkey, Germany's old allies from the First World War, likewise again aligned themselves with Germany.

Hitler, therefore, had realized the first political vision of his youth – a Greater Germany as the dominating power over all the successor states of the old Austria and, in addition, of the entire area between Germany/Austria and Russia. He had achieved all this without a war, with the full agreement of Britain and France, while Russia had to watch this massive build-up of power on its Western frontier, suspiciously but impotently. All that remained to be done to consolidate this new Greater German East European empire was to give it a shape and to give its nations time to get used to their new condition. There was no longer any need for a war, and that it should be accomplished without any war was also the tacit condition upon which Britain and France had given their agreement. After all, they wanted to buy 'peace in our time' at Munich, and when, upon his return from Munich, the British Prime Minister Chamberlain proclaimed this goal as attained – rashly, as it was to turn out – , he did so because he believed that Hitler would now be engaged in peaceful pursuits for years to come. After all, the organization and consolidation of the huge and heterogeneous East European zone of influence, which Chamberlain together with his French colleague Daladier had made available to Germany in Munich, demanded two things, apart from tact and sensitivity: constructive statesmanship – one might say state-building skill – and patience.

But Hitler lacked just these two qualities. We have come across his lack of skill in matters of constructive statesmanship before. After all, since he had not even been able or willing to give a new constitutional system to his own existing state, how could he be expected to do it for a community of states yet to be created. Hitler quite simply lacked the statesmanlike vision this would have required and, strange to say, he was not interested in the fate of the countries and nations now placed in his hands. To him they were merely auxiliary nations, suppliers of raw materials and deployment areas for his further adventures.

He did not have the patience that would have been needed for organizing his new Great Empire, in fact a life task. Ever since 1925 at the latest he had a far greater goal – the conquest and subjection of Russia, following the preliminary elimination of France. And, as we have seen, he was in a hurry because he wanted to realize all his ideas within his own lifetime. In April 1939 he was fifty, and we may recall his remark, already quoted: 'I am now fifty; I would rather have the war now than when I

am fifty-five or sixty.' Actually he would have liked the war as
early as 1938 – we have quoted that admission, too, in a different
context. The Munich Agreement, which friend and foe rightly
viewed as a fabulous triumph for Hitler, he himself regarded as
a downright defeat. Things had not gone the way he had wanted.
He had been compelled to accept from the hands of Britain and
France what he would have preferred to take by force, and he had
lost time. So in 1939 he made sure he got the war that had escaped
him in 1938. Through the totally unnecessary military occupation
and further partitioning of a helpless, softened-up and truncated
Czechoslovakia he destroyed the basis of the Munich Agreement,
and when Britain and France thereupon concluded or renewed
an alliance with Poland he courted war with Poland with a
certain bravado and thereby provoked Britain's and France's
declaration of war.

This declaration of war was not yet war itself. Neither Britain
nor France was ready in 1939 for active war with Germany, either
materially or psychologically; they left it to Hitler to wage war
against them. For this war he was ready as far as France was
concerned, but *not* as far as Britain was concerned. France's
'annihilation', after all, had always figured in Hitler's plans as a
prelude to his real war against Russia for living space. The campaign in France in 1940 that followed actually was his greatest
success.

Hitler intended that Britain should play the part of an ally or
at least of a benevolent neutral. He had made no preparations for
an invasion of England or for a naval war of blockade against
Britain on the high seas. He shied away from an improvised
invasion, probably rightly in view of British superiority on the sea
and in the air. Terror bombing proved a poor means of making
Britain grow weary of the war; if anything it was counter-
productive. Thus, from the summer of 1940, Hitler had the un-
decided, unsought-for war with Britain hanging round his neck, a
first indication that his policy of 1938/39 had been mistaken.

At the same time, he had defeated France, which gave him an
aura of irresistibility throughout Europe, and he had, moreover,

militarily occupied the entire Western continent from the North Cape down to the Pyrenees. And this offered him once more the chance which the Munich Agreement had offered him for Eastern Europe only – the chance of giving the whole of continental Europe a 'New Order' and ensuring permanent German predominance in Europe. The chance was not only offering itself, it positively thrust itself on him: after all, he had just fought a victorious war, which would have been fought in vain without the conclusion of a peace. What was more, France showed itself more than willing to make peace; indeed some of its politicians now in government were even ready for an alliance. What they were expressly offering they christened 'collaboration' – an exceedingly elastic concept. If Hitler had only wished it, he could have had peace with France at any time in the summer of 1940, and if that peace had turned out to be reasonably generous it would, without any doubt, have made all the lesser Western European countries against whom Hitler had made war equally hungry for peace. Conclusion of peace with France, followed by a European peace congress called if possible jointly with France, from which a kind of European league of states or at least a defensive and economic community might have emerged – all that was within reach for a German statesman in Hitler's position in the summer of 1940. It would, incidentally, have been the most promising approach to disarming Britain psychologically and letting the war with Britain wither away. After all, what would Britain have left to fight for if the countries for whose sake it had declared war were making their own peace with Hitler? And what could Britain have done against a unified Europe united around Germany?

It is significant that these opportunities can be shown not to have played the least part in Hitler's thinking and planning during the twelve months from June 1940 to June 1941. He did not even consider them in order to reject them. Such a policy simply never occurred to him. When, after his victorious campaign in France, he made an offer of peace it was not addressed to vanquished France but to undefeated Britain – a totally paradoxical attitude if one stops to think about it. Britain had only just declared war. It had only just begun to mobilize its forces and reserves, which it was able to do at its own pace since its naval and air forces were protecting it against invasion. From its point of view none of the reasons for the war had been eliminated. On the contrary, they had been multiplied by Hitler's new wars of aggression and his occupation of Norway and Denmark, of Holland, Belgium and Luxembourg. Why should it make peace? The vanquished may seek peace, not the undefeated.

Wars are fought in order to make one's opponent ready to make peace through military victory; if one fails to make use of that readiness then one has thrown away one's military victory. Hitler threw away his victory over defeated France, a France ready to make peace, and instead addressed an offer of peace to undefeated Britain which was by no means ready to make peace; and he did so, incidentally, without any hints of concessions on the controversial points which had led to war with Britain. That was an incomprehensible elementary political mistake. The fact that, together with his victory over France, he also threw away his chance of uniting Europe, a chance never to return, and of making it accept Germany's hegemony through such unification, magnified that mistake to gigantic proportions. It is odd that, even today, this gigantic mistake still scarcely figures in the literature on Hitler.

It is, of course, oddly impossible to visualize Hitler as a generous victor and a farsighted patient peacemaker. In his last broadcast, on 30 January 1945, he described himself as a man 'who always knew only one thing: strike, strike and strike again' – a self-characterization intended as self-praise but in reality a self-accusation, maybe even an exaggerated one. Hitler not only knew how to be violent, he knew also how to be cunning. But it is true that he never understood the wisdom of Cromwell's dictum that one does not really possess what one only possesses by force; he was no peacemaker, this was a talent he lacked. Perhaps that is the reason why the fantastic chance which he missed in the summer of 1940 is scarcely ever adequately mentioned in most accounts of Hitler and the Second World War. But it is at the same time, a reason for stopping the film just then, in the summer of 1940, long enough to assess Hitler's strengths and weaknesses. At no other single time can they be viewed together so completely.

After all, Hitler had himself created the opportunity which he threw away. He had, without any doubt, proved himself a paragon of willpower, energy and vigour. He had brought into play all the (by no means negligible) political gifts he possessed – above all an infallible sense of the hidden weaknesses of an opponent and an ability to exploit such weaknesses in an 'icily-cold' manner and by 'lightning-quick' decisions ('icily-cold' and 'lightning-quick' were favourite expressions of his). In addition, as he had likewise proved at that historical moment, he possessed a rare combination of political and military gifts. What, on the other hand, he lacked totally was the constructive imagination of the statesman, the ability to build enduring structures. That was why he was unable to realize a peace treaty – just as he had been unable earlier to produce a constitution at home (after all, peace treaties are to the community of states what constitutions are to the individual state). What also prevented him was his reluctance to commit himself and his impatience, both these qualities being connected with his self-adulation. Since he regarded himself as infallible and blindly trusted his 'intuition', he could not create institutions which would have placed fetters on it; and since he regarded himself as irreplaceable and was absolutely determined to accomplish his entire programme in his own lifetime, he could not plant anything that needed time to grow. He could not leave anything to his successors. He could not even bring himself to make sure of the succession. (Indeed the idea of successors always seemed strangely disagreeable to him.)

These were flaws of character and lack of talents. In addition, however, the fateful omissions of 1940 are also due to erroneous thinking by Hitler the 'programmatician', to misconceptions we have already discussed in the chapter under that heading.

To Hitler the political thinker war was the norm and peace the exception. He realized that peace could serve the preparation of a war. What he did not realize was that war must always serve the conclusion of a peace. To Hitler the ultimate goal of all politics was a victorious war – not the peace thereby won. He had spent six years preparing the war while uttering assurances of peaceful intentions. Now that he had his war he could not relinquish it in a hurry. On some occasions he actually said so. He said that if after the victorious wars against Poland and France he were to allow an intermediate state of peace then it would not prove so easy to 'rouse' Germany to a new war against Russia.

There was yet another reason why Hitler was not open to the idea of a peace with France in particular. In his political thinking, as we saw in the preceding chapter, the victory of the stronger invariably meant 'the annihilation of the weak or his unconditional submission'. It is in connection with France in particular that in *Mein Kampf* the word 'annihilation' appears in a certain matter-of-course way. 'The eternal, in itself so unprofitable, struggle between us and France', we read, could make sense only 'on condition that Germany regards the annihilation of France really as just the means of subsequently giving to our nation, at long last, the possibility of expansion elsewhere'. In the circumstances of the summer of 1940, when Hitler was still hoping that Britain might give in, the policy of annihilation that Hitler was then already practising in Poland and would introduce in Russia the following year was clearly not possible in France. But Hitler obviously could not envisage any other war aim for France but annihilation, and that was why his mind was particularly closed to a peace with France which, to be useful, would have had to be a peace of reconciliation and indeed of unification. The idea of annihilation had not been dropped; its realization had merely been put off, or at any rate left open. At least, Hitler did not want to block any options in that respect.

We find here strangely combined two of Hitler's traits which, at first glance, might seem to contradict each other, his reluctance to commit himself and his programmatic stubbornness. The two together made him, up to a point, blind to realities. He failed to see unprogrammed opportunities just as he failed to see unexpected dangers threatening his programme. That is where he differed from Stalin with whom he shared a lot of characteristics (including the cruelty with which we shall have to concern ourselves in the next chapter). Stalin always kept an alert eye for the realities surrounding him. Hitler trusted himself to move mountains.

Nowhere is all this more clearly revealed than during the year from June 1940 to June 1941, the year in which Hitler without knowing it decided his fate. He failed to see that he had attained all that was attainable. He was not interested in the fact that a continental European peace, which was then due, would have been bound to starve Britain's resolution. Indeed, he was not really interested in the war against Britain at all: it had not been part of the plan, and it did not fit into Hitler's picture of the world. That America was drawing menacingly closer behind Britain, Hitler for a long time refused to take seriously. He relied on America's backwardness in armaments, on the domestic disunity between interventionists and isolationists, and, at the worst, on America being diverted by Japan. In his own programme of action America did not figure. Instead this programme envisaged that after the preliminary war against France to free his rear would come the great main war, the 'war for living space' against Russia. After some hesitation Hitler eventually decided in favour of that war, even though in the programme Britain had been scheduled not as an enemy but as an ally or a benevolent neutral spectator in the German–Russian war. He made the decision despite the fact that in this unscheduled war which he now had on his hands against Britain Russia was indispensable as a blockade-running supplier of raw materials and foodstuffs, and indeed had loyally proved itself in that role. This latter consideration Hitler brushed aside with the argument that a conquered Russia would prove an even more reliable supplier of raw materials and foodstuffs. As for Britain, he persuaded himself that Britain would give up the war as hopeless as soon as its hopes of having Russia as a future ally were dashed. He did not seem to notice that Russia was not giving the slightest encouragement to such British hopes and that Britain evidently was relying not on Russia but on America as a future ally.

One should not take these rationalization attempts of Hitler's too seriously. His attack against Russia was made not *because* but *in spite of* the continuing war against Britain; nor did it arise from the friction with Russia which had developed during the second half of 1940 and was eased by the summer of 1941. It arose quite simply because Russia had always been marked on Hitler's mental map as German living space, and because in Hitler's timetable the moment had now come, following his victory over France, to ring up the curtain over this main number in his programme of conquests. Hitler had allowed his generals to gauge this intention of his as early as July 1940. On 18 December 1940 it was elevated to a firm decision and on 22 June 1941 it was translated into reality.

That Hitler's unprovoked attack against Russia was a mistake – and, moreover, a mistake which of itself determined the outcome of the war – is patent to everyone today. What is left to decide is whether that mistake was discernible as a mistake at the time. Russia was universally underestimated in 1941 – the British and American General Staff, too, anticipated a rapid Russian defeat – and Russia itself, by its poor performance in the winter war against Finland in 1939, had given ground for that assessment. The impressive initial successes of the 1941 campaign seemed to confirm Hitler's low opinion of Russia's power of resistance. Whether he could have taken Moscow with a different strategy is still a matter of controversy. He certainly got very close to doing so.

But even the fall of Moscow, given Russia's vast reserves of manpower and space, would not have ended the war in 1941 any more than it did in 1812. How, in point of fact, was a war against Russia to be concluded at all, in view of those reserves of human beings and space? Oddly enough, as we now know, Hitler never seriously posed this question to himself, just as in the case of France he never thought beyond military victory. His war plan envisaged no more, even in the event of military victory, than an advance to a line from Archangel to Astrakhan. In other words, he would have remained saddled with an enormous eastern front at a time when his war against Britain was still going on and war with America was threatening.

In the meantime the war against Britain and the subjection of an occupied but not pacified continent tied down one-quarter of the German Army, one-third of the Luftwaffe and the whole of the Navy, as well as the corresponding supply industries. Moreover, the unfinished war in the West was imposing a strict time limit on the war in the East. Britain, lagging years behind Germany in armaments at the beginning of the war, was growing steadily stronger, as was America, and within two or at the latest three years both would be able to take the offensive in Europe. All these were reasons which surely would have made a responsible head of state hesitate about starting a war against Russia in the conditions of 1941 – a war which no one was compelling him to wage. But Hitler was answerable only to himself and his intuition had been telling him for the past fifteen years, ever since he wrote down this assessment in *Mein Kampf*, that 'the gigantic empire in the east' was 'ripe for collapse'. He trusted his intuition so blindly that he did not even make provisions for winter equipment for the German Army. He was convinced that the campaign which had started on 22 June would be victoriously concluded before the winter. Instead, the onset of winter, as is well known, brought him his first serious German defeat on the outskirts of Moscow. And the War Diary of the Wehrmacht Operations Staff commented on it: 'When the disaster of the winter of 1941/42 broke, the Führer . . . realized that from this point of culmination onwards . . . no victory could any longer be won.' That was on 6 December 1941. On 11 December Hitler declared war on America.

That was the crowning mistake, the one which, just because it is so spectacular, is still the most inexplicable of the mistakes with which Hitler in 1941 dug his own grave. It is almost as if he had drawn from the realization that with the failure of his *Blitzkrieg* against Russia victory had become impossible the conclusion of now coveting defeat – and of making that defeat as complete and disastrous as possible. Surely the fact that defeat would be inevitable once the (even then) strongest power on earth was added to his undefeated opponents Britain and Russia cannot possibly have escaped Hitler.

There is to this day no comprehensible rational explanation for what one is tempted to describe as an act of lunacy. Consider: the declaration of war was in practice a mere invitation to America to wage war against Germany. For Hitler possessed no means of conducting an active war against America, not even long-range bombers which might have administered the odd pinprick. With that invitation to war Hitler did the American President Roosevelt the greatest possible favour: for more than a year Roosevelt had been trying through more and more open support for Britain and eventually with small acts of real war in the Atlantic, to provoke Hitler into war. Roosevelt, among all Hitler's opponents, was the only one who undoubtedly desired war because he regarded it as necessary, but in view of the opposition within his own country he could not start it himself. Hitler had, most sensibly, refused to be provoked for more than a year. On the contrary, he had done everything to divert America from participation in the European war by encouraging and supporting Japan in adopting a threatening attitude towards America. And that policy of diversion had just achieved its greatest success: on 7 December Japan, by its attack on the US Pacific Fleet at Pearl Harbour had started a war against the United States. If Germany continued to keep quiet, how could Roosevelt, with his country now so seriously challenged by Japan, mobilize it against Germany when Germany had not done anything to the USA? How could he have explained this to the American people? By declaring war on him Hitler saved him the trouble. Why?

Was it 'Nibelung loyalty' to Japan? This cannot be seriously considered. There was no obligation for Germany to participate in any war which Japan started on its own account and vice versa. The German–Japanese–Italian Triple Alliance of September

1940 was purely defensive. Accordingly, Japan had not taken part in Germany's war of aggression against Russia. On the contrary, when the German deployment against Russia became unmistakable in April 1941 Japan had concluded a neutrality pact with Russia, which it carefully observed; and it was Siberian troops, pulled back from the Russo-Japanese military frontier in Manchuria, that halted the German offensive at Moscow. Hitler would have been entirely justified, not only legally but also morally, in regarding Japan's war against America as the welcome diversion and relief that it could have been for Germany, and in adopting the role of the coolly smiling observer that Japan was adopting *vis-à-vis* the German war against Russia. Moreover he could do nothing to give Japan any kind of active assistance. And surely it hardly needs saying that he was not a man to let his policy be influenced by sentimental feelings of loyalty, least of all towards Japan.

No, what induced Hitler to trigger off America's entry into the German war, an entry which he had so far sensibly done everything to prevent, was not the Japanese attack on Pearl Harbour but the successful Russian counter-offensive at Moscow which, as is attested, led Hitler to the intuitive realization 'that no victory could any longer be won'. That much can be said with some measure of certainty. But it does not by itself explain Hitler's step. Even viewed as an act of desperation his declaration of war on America does not really make sense.

Was that declaration of war a disguised cry for help? The situation in Russia in December 1941 presaged two likelihoods, one of which the further course of the war was to confirm. The first was that Russia, with its more than 200 millions, was quite simply stronger than Germany with its 80 millions, and that this superior strength was bound to prevail in the long run. The second likelihood was an instant Napoleonic disaster under the double effect of the Russian offensive and the Russian winter. Largely by Hitler's determination this was narrowly averted. In view of this possibility it might be conceivable that Hitler positively wished to bring about an Anglo-American invasion in the

West, so that he would, at least, lose not to Russia but to the Western Powers at whose hands a defeated Germany might expect more lenient treatment. But against this conjecture stands the fact that three years later when matters really had reached the point where Germany was only left with the option of receiving the fatal blow in the West or in the East, Hitler chose the East, a point we shall have to discuss under the heading 'Betrayal'. There is also the fact that Hitler was well informed about the state of American mobilization and American backwardness in armaments: in the winter of 1941/42 the Western Powers, with the best will in the world, were not ready for invasion, the Americans even less so than the British.

Or did Hitler hope that by creating a US–British–Russian coalition, which could only be a highly unnatural one, he might sow discord among his enemies? Did he, more especially, believe that America in particular would soon find itself in conflict with Russia, a conflict which he might then exploit in order to pull his head out of the noose? In a situation in which 'no victory could any longer be won' this might be a speculative but by no means entirely unrealistic consideration. In point of fact, Russia and Britain/America repeatedly did have very serious quarrels in the subsequent course of the war, in 1942 and 1943 about the 'Second Front in Europe'; in 1943 and 1944 about Poland; and finally in 1945 about Germany (though in these quarrels Churchill's Britain was the much more stubborn antagonist of Stalin's Russia than Roosevelt's America). What was later to become the 'Cold War' certainly began to take shape during the Second World War, and no prophetic gift was needed in 1941 to expect such a development. But when it did arise, Hitler did nothing to exploit it. A separate peace with Russia on a *status quo* basis, which he might have got in 1942 and perhaps even in 1943 (when the Russians, bleeding from a thousand wounds, were bearing virtually the whole burden of the war and clamouring in vain for a second front in Europe), was emphatically rejected by Hitler. As for the possibility of a peace with the West, he threw away any chance of it by his monstrous crimes during just those years after 1941.

In looking for the motive behind Hitler's inexplicable declaration of war on America one is confined to suppositions since he never revealed it himself. That declaration of war is not only the most incomprehensible of the mistakes by which during 1940 and 1941 he transformed near-complete victory into inevitable defeat, but also the most lonely of his lonely decisions. Until he made this declaration at a Reichstag meeting specially called for the purpose, he had discussed it with no other person, neither with the generals of his military entourage with whom, since the beginning of the war in Russia, he spent the major part of his days, nor with his Foreign Minister, nor even with his Government Cabinet which he had not called since 1938. But he did make some strange remarks, which were recorded, to two foreign visitors, the Danish Foreign Minister Scavenius and the Croatian Foreign Minister Lorković. This was on 27 November when the Russian counter-offensive had not even yet begun but the German offensive towards Moscow had been halted. 'On this point, too, I am icily cold,' he had said. 'If one day the German nation is no longer sufficiently strong or sufficiently ready for sacrifice to stake its own blood for its existence, then let it perish and be annihilated by some other stronger power . . . In that case I shall shed no tears for the German nation.' Eerie words. In point of fact, Hitler in 1945 did give orders for anything that was still standing in Germany to be blown up and for the German nation to be deprived of any chance of survival, in other words to be punished by annihilation for having proved incapable of conquering the world. Even in 1941, at the first setback, that thought of betrayal suddenly emerged. And it is in tune with a trait in Hitler's character that we have already come across, his inclination towards drawing the most radical conclusions – always 'icily cold' and 'lightning-quick'. Was the declaration of war on America the first hint that Hitler had inwardly changed gear? Had he decided that if he could not go down in history as the greatest conqueror he would at least be the architect of the greatest catastrophe?

One thing is certain. With his declaration of war on America Hitler sealed the defeat which was heralded in the Battle of

Moscow, and from 1942 onwards he did nothing to avert it. He developed no more new political or military initiatives. The inventiveness which one could not deny him during the preceding years was as if swept away after 1942. Political opportunities which still offered themselves for somehow wriggling out from the lost war remained disregarded as did even military opportunities of still turning the fortunes of war, such as Rommel's surprise victories in Africa in the summer of 1942. It was as though Hitler was no longer interested in victory but in something different.

It is also worth noting that during those years Hitler became increasingly withdrawn. He was no longer seen or heard. No more contacts with the masses, no visits to the front, no glances at cities stricken by bombing, hardly a public speech. Hitler was living entirely at his military headquarters. There, it is true, he was still the ruler, as absolute as ever, dismissing and replacing generals and taking all military decisions himself – often odd decisions such as the sacrifice of the Sixth Army at Stalingrad. His strategy during those years was stubborn and unimaginative; his only recipe was: 'Hold out at any price'. The price was paid – but there was no holding out. The conquered territories were lost piece by piece, in the East from the end of 1942, and from 1944 in the West also. Hitler did not react; he was conducting a protracted war of hanging on, no longer for victory but for time. But if he had never had time before, why was he fighting for it now?

Hitler had always had two goals – Germany's domination over Europe and the extermination of the Jews. He had failed in the former. Now he concentrated on the latter. While the German armies were fighting their long, costly and fruitless war of delay, day after day the trains with human freight were rolling towards the extermination camps. The order for the 'Final Solution of the Jewish Problem' had been given in January 1942.

During the years leading up to 1941 Hitler had made the world catch its breath by his political and military deeds. That was now over. What made the world catch its breath now were his crimes.

Crimes

HERE is no doubt that Hitler is a figure of world political history; there is equally no doubt that he belongs in the annals of crime. He attempted, albeit unsuccessfully, to establish an empire by wars of conquest. Such an enterprise invariably involves a lot of bloodshed; nevertheless, no one would describe the great conquerors, from Alexander to Napoleon, simply as criminals. Hitler is not a criminal merely because he followed in their footsteps.

He is a criminal for a totally different reason. Hitler had countless harmless people put to death, for no military or political purpose, but merely for his personal gratification. In that respect he belongs not with Alexander or Napoleon but rather with such killers as Crippen and Christie, though with the difference that he accomplished on a conveyor belt basis what they did as craftsmen, so that his victims are counted not in dozens or hundreds but in millions. He was, among other things, quite simply a mass murderer.

Here we are using the term in its precise criminological meaning, not by any means in the rhetorical or polemical sense in which it is sometimes flung in the face of statesmen or generals who send their enemies or their own troops to death. Statesmen (and generals) have at all times and in all countries found themselves in the situation of ordering people to be killed – in war, in civil war, in national crises and at times of revolution. That does not make them criminals. It may be true that nations have always been very sensitive to whether, in committing those deeds, their rulers were only obeying necessity or secretly enjoying themselves. The reputation of *cruel* rulers has always remained tainted even if otherwise they were efficient rulers. This goes, for instance, for Stalin. Hitler, among other things, was also a cruel ruler – which, incidentally, made him something of an exception in German history. Prior to Hitler cruel rulers were far less common in Germany than, for instance, in Russia or France. But this is not the point here. Hitler was cruel not only as a ruler or conqueror. What is special about Hitler is that he had murders committed, and on an unimaginable scale, even when the national interest provided not the slightest reason or even pretext for them. Sometimes, indeed, his mass murders were actually counter to his political and military interests. Thus he might possibly have been able to win the war against Russia politically – a war which, as we now know, could never have been won militarily – if he had appeared as a liberator instead of an exterminator. But his lust for murder was even stronger than his by no means slight ability for political calculation.

Hitler's mass murders were committed during the war but they were not acts of war. On the contrary, it may be said that he used the war as a pretext for committing mass murders which had nothing to do with the war, but for which he had always felt a personal need. 'If the best men were killed at the front,' he had written in *Mein Kampf*, 'then at home one could at least exterminate the vermin.' The extermination of those human beings who were vermin to Hitler was related to the war only in the sense that the war diverted attention from it. Otherwise it was, to Hitler, an end in itself and in no way a means to victory or the averting of defeat.

On the contrary, it impeded the conduct of the war because thousands of ss men, who were fit for active service but who were engaged on this operation, were lacking at the front – all in all the equivalent of several divisions – , and because the daily mass transports to the extermination camps, right across Europe, were depriving the fighting forces of an appreciable amount of rolling stock which was in short supply and which was urgently needed for supplies. And once victory could no longer be won, the murder operations rendered impossible any compromise peace because as the facts became increasingly known they convinced the statesmen, first in the West and then also in Russia, that the war could be meaningfully concluded not by any diplomatic transaction *with* Hitler but only by court action *against* him. The war aim of 'punishment of those responsible for the crimes', proclaimed by the Western Allies in January 1942 and eventually also by the

Soviet Union in November 1943, entailed the further war aim of unconditional surrender.

During the years from 1942 to 1945 there was a widespread realization throughout the world that Hitler's mass murders were not merely 'war crimes' but crimes pure and simple, and moreover crimes on an unprecedented scale; a civilizational disaster which, in a sense, began where the usual 'war crimes' ended. Unfortunately that awareness was later blurred by the Nuremberg 'war crime trials', an unfortunate performance which no one now likes to remember.

The justice of the victors had many shortcomings: the principal defendant was absent, having removed himself from all earthly justice; the law underlying the trials was retrospective *ad hoc* law; worst of all, Hitler's real crime, the production-line mass extermination of Poles, Russians, Jews, Gipsies and invalids was only a marginal charge, bracketed with compulsory labour and deportation as 'crimes against humanity', while the principal charges were those of 'crimes against peace', i.e. war as such, and 'war crimes', defined as 'violations of the laws and usages of war'.

Such violations, needless to say, had occurred on all sides to a more or less serious extent, and of course the war itself had also been conducted by the victorious powers. It was therefore easy to claim that here was a case of guilty men judging guilty men, and that the defendants were in fact being condemned for having lost the war. (Field-Marshal Montgomery publicly expressed this idea after the trial.) Nuremberg has caused a great deal of confusion. Among Germans – and more particularly *those* Germans who had most reason to reflect and be ashamed – it has given rise to a compensation mentality, an attitude that counters any accusation with a ready 'tu quoque' – and what about yourselves? Hitler's real crimes, which thirty-five years ago made the blood run cold in people's veins, now have to be laboriously picked out from among what one might call the normal dirt of war. The best starting point perhaps would be to examine those of Hitler's misdeeds which do *not* come under the heading of these crimes, at the risk that some readers might regard this as a whitewashing of Hitler. In fact it is the reverse.

Let us begin with the 'crime against peace'. In the Nuremberg Trials, for the first and so far the only time, war as such (or at least a planned and deliberate war of aggression) was declared a crime. Some people at the time actually regarded the 'crime against peace' as the most important charge of the indictment, one that basically embraced all the others; they hailed the listing of war as a crime as an epoch-making forward step by mankind. This view is not often encountered nowadays. War and murder, easy though it is to equate them rhetorically, are two different things. This can be demonstrated especially in the case of Hitler.

Attitudes towards war, at least among the Western nations, have changed considerably in this century. War used to be glorified. Even when the First World War began, the people involved – and not only the Germans – embarked on it with jubilation and enthusiasm. That is a thing of the past. The Second World War was felt by all nations – not excluding the Germans – as a misfortune and a scourge. Since then the development of weapons of mass destruction has further intensified a general horror, revulsion and fear of war. But it has not abolished war. A way to abolish war has yet to be discovered. To pronounce it a crime, as was done at Nuremberg, is no such way. This is witnessed by the many wars which have since taken place and are still taking place, and by the enormous efforts and sums of money which those very powers, who at Nuremberg declared war to be a crime, are investing year by year in order to remain prepared for war. They cannot do otherwise, for they know that war is still possible and that in certain circumstances it may become unavoidable.

Even before the Second World War, most of the states which were to become involved in it had solemnly signed a renunciation of war in the Kellogg Pact, and similar renunciations of war have, since 1945, been part and parcel of international instruments, from the United Nations Charter to the Helsinki Agreement. But every government knows that when it comes to the crunch, it cannot rely on them and therefore makes appropriate arrangements. No one would for that reason declare all governments to be gangs of criminals. To call something that is disagreeable but unavoidable a crime does not help. One might just as well call defecation a crime. The most cursory glance at world history shows that war can no more be banished from the system of states than defecation can from the biological system of the human body, and the simplest reflection will show why this is so. Wars are fought between states, and are part of the state system because, and as long as, states are the ultimate level of power and force existing on Earth. Their power monopoly is indispensable; it is a necessary prerequisite if internal group and class conflicts among their citizens are to be settled non-violently. At the same time, however, this makes it inevitable that conflicts between states themselves, in the extreme case, will be settled violently, i.e. by war. Things would only be different if, above the states, there were to be a higher level of power, a single universal government ruling the whole world, with the states being subordinate to it in the way that the members of a federation are to a federal state. Although such a world government has always been the ideal of the great conquerors and of the vast empires founded by them, the objective has never so far been achieved. So long as the political world consists of a multitude of sovereign states Schiller's lines will continue to be valid:

Yes, war is terrible, like heaven's scourges, but it is good, it too is Destiny . . .

To label war a crime, as was attempted at Nuremberg, can only make it more terrible because the loser is then bound to fight not for victory or defeat but for life or death.

It might be objected that not every war was labelled a crime at Nuremberg but only wars of aggression and conquest. That Hitler conducted that kind of war, at least in the East, no one will dispute. Unlike the First World War, there is hardly any controversy about who was responsible for the Second World War.

Hitler planned, willed and fought that war with the short-term aim of establishing a German-dominated Greater Reich and the long-term aim of world domination. But even that cannot simply be described as a crime, particularly if one believes that war should be abolished because mankind can no longer, at its present level of technology, afford to tolerate war.

If in a world of sovereign states wars are inevitable and if, at the same time, they have in our technological age become a threat to the survival of mankind, then a 'war to end war' seems to lie in the logic of the human situation. For, as we have just seen, a world government would be the only sure means of abolishing war as an institution, and there is probably no other way of establishing a world government than by a successful war of world conquest. Our lessons from history, at least, reveal no other way.

It is obvious that institutions such as the League of Nations in Geneva or the United Nations in New York cannot abolish war. On the other hand, the longest and most secure peace that we know of, the Pax Romana of the first four centuries of our era, had been preceded by a whole string of deliberate Roman wars of conquest, and had only been made possible by them. Imperium Romanum and Pax Romana were the same thing. To quote a smaller but historically closer instance: throughout the centuries there had repeatedly been wars among the German states, including such devastating ones as the Thirty Years' War, until Bismarck united Germany – through war. And what about the Second World War itself? Did it not, for the two principal victorious powers, Russia and America, ultimately become a war of conquest and the foundation of empires? Are not NATO and the Warsaw Pact in a sense American and Russian empires? Was not the Cold War, which succeeded the Second World War until it was temporarily stifled by the nuclear stalemate, already a silent war for world rule? And does one not have to concede that the Russian and American spheres of domination, which emerged as the result of the Second World War, are today the only parts of the world within which there is secure peace? It may sound paradoxical, but the successful conquerors and founders of empires, of whom Hitler wished to become one, have throughout history done more for peace than all the paper renunciations of war. Hitler's crime, therefore, does not lie in the fact that he wished to emulate them – or, in other words, that he tried unsuccessfully to accomplish what his American and Russian conquerors, set in motion by him, later achieved successfully.

Nor does Hitler's particular crime lie in the 'violations of the laws and usages of war', i.e. the 'war crimes' proper which gave the Nuremberg Trials their name. To begin with, it should be made clear that this point of the indictment is in conflict with the one just discussed. If war as such is regarded as a crime then its laws and usages are part of that crime and it does not then matter whether they are violated. In point of fact, the 'laws and usages of war' are based upon the contrary view that war is not a crime but a basically accepted (because unavoidable) international institution; they merely serve the 'hedging in of war', and attempt, chiefly by regulations and agreements on the protection of civilian populations and prisoners of war, to contain it and make it more tolerable.

Besides, they are anything but complete. The Geneva Convention, which protects life and limb of prisoners of war, has not been ratified by all states. The Hague Land War Rules, which prohibit acts of violence against the civilian population in the theatre of war, are not matched by any Air War Rules; bombing raids on residential areas, in consequence, do not run counter to the universally accepted laws and usages of war.

More importantly, infringements of the various laws and usages of war, which of course occur in all wars on all sides, are not traditionally subject to international sanctions, and for good reasons. Those responsible are punished, with varying severity, during the war itself by superiors or court martial of the offender's own side – sometimes with great severity since looting, murder, rape, etc. must, if tolerated, undermine the discipline and hence the fighting value of one's own forces. After the war, however, such war crimes, if still unpunished, are usually silently amnestied on all sides – and only judicial fanatics can deplore that. There is wisdom in treating the, as it were, normal horrors of war as concomitant phenomena of an inevitable exceptional situation, one in which decent citizens and family men necessarily get accustomed to killing, and in allowing them to sink into oblivion as quickly as possible once the war is over.

It was an error on the part of the victorious powers after the Second World War to disregard that wisdom, not merely because prosecution of only the vanquished for excesses which had been perpetrated also by the victors was bound to give rise to a sense of injustice, but also because lumping together Hitler's crimes with the more usual kind of war crimes blunted people's understanding of their exceptional nature. The important point about Hitler's mass murders is the very fact that they were *not* war crimes. A massacre of prisoners of war in the confusion and heat of battle; the execution of hostages in a war against partisans; the bombing of purely residential areas in the 'strategic' air war; the sinking of passenger liners and neutral ships in the U-boat war – all these are war crimes, undoubtedly frightful, but by general consent best forgotten by everybody once the war is over. Mass murder, the systematic extermination of entire population groups, 'the extermination of vermin' committed against humans, is something else entirely.

It is with these crimes of Hitler that we now have to concern ourselves. I intend to spare the reader the description of the horrible details. They are amply described in other books, for instance in Reinhard Henkys's accurately documented account *Die Nationalsozialistischen Gewaltverbrechen*. We shall confine ourselves here to setting out the facts in chronological sequence.

1. Hitler's written order for the mass killing of invalids in Germany bears the date of 1 September 1939, the day of the outbreak of war. On the strength of this order roughly 100,000 Germans – 'useless eaters' – were officially put to death over the next two years. In detail these were 70,000 to 80,000 patients in medical and nursing institutions, 10,000 to 20,000 segregated invalids and disabled people in concentration camps, all the Jewish patients in psychiatric hospitals, and roughly 3,000

children between the ages of three and thirteen, mainly in special schools or requiring special care. The operation was suspended in August 1941, partly because it had been causing growing disquiet among the population and had given rise to public protests from the Churches, and partly – perhaps chiefly – because the organization set up for the implementation of the liquidation of the sick (code name T4) was needed by Hitler for the extermination of the Jews which was then being launched on a major scale. Later there was no opportunity for resuming the extermination of the sick.

2. The extermination of the gipsies likewise began in Germany in September 1939. They were being rounded up everywhere and first moved to concentration camps and then, in two operations, in 1941 and 1943, transferred to extermination camps. From 1941 onwards the gipsies in the occupied countries of Eastern Europe were being as systematically liquidated as the Jews living there. This mass murder – perhaps because it had never been heralded or accompanied by propaganda but had taken place quietly – has scarcely been researched in detail even now. It was not talked about while it was taking place, and to this day we do not know much more about it than that it did take place. Records are scarce. Estimates of the total numbers murdered go as high as 500,000. At any rate of the 25,000 gipsies living in Germany in 1939 only about 5,000 were alive in 1945.

3. About one month later, in October 1939, following the termination of military operations in Poland, Hitler's third series of mass murders began. This time the victims were the Polish intelligentsia and leading strata of society. This operation continued throughout five long years. Here we have no written order by Hitler – the written order for the extermination of the sick was the last of its kind – but only verbal instructions which, however, are equally well attested and were equally strictly implemented. Heydrich, for instance, in a report dated 2 July 1940 on complaints from the Wehrmacht (the armed forces) about the German reign of terror in Poland, refers to an 'extraordinarily radical special order of the Führer' (e.g. an order to liquidate numerous

Polish leading classes, running into thousands of people), and the Governor-General of occupied Poland, Frank, quotes a verbal reminder by Hitler dated 30 May 1940: 'Whatever leading stratum we have now identified in Poland must be liquidated; whatever moves up into its place must be secured by us and again removed after an appropriate space of time.' It is an established fact that, upon Hitler's instructions, throughout the next five years not only Jews but also non-Jewish Poles were stripped of their rights and put at the mercy of totally arbitrary rule, and that in particular the members of the educated classes – priests, teachers, professors, journalists, entrepreneurs – fell victim to a systematic campaign of eradication. Its aims can be gauged from a memorandum of Himmler of May 1940 (Himmler was Hitler's right-hand man throughout all his crimes, and may therefore be regarded also as his Führer's mouthpiece in these matters):

> For the non-German population of the East there shall be no school higher than the four-year elementary school. The objective of that elementary school shall be merely this: simple arithmetic up to no more than 500, writing of one's name, the lesson that it is a divine commandment to be obedient to the Germans and to be honest, hardworking and well-behaved. I do not consider reading to be necessary. Aside from that school there shall be no school whatever in the East ... The population of the Government-General, following the consistent implementation of these measures, will necessarily consist, after the next ten years, of a residual inferior population ... That population will be available as a leaderless working mass and will provide Germany each year with itinerant workers and with labour for special projects (roads, quarries, construction).

Such a de-civilization of an ancient cultured nation was, of course, in itself a crime, but, moreover, it included the mass murder of Poland's educated classes. The precise number of educated Poles who fell victim to this systematic mass murder is more difficult to establish than that of the murdered Jews. Alto-

gether, according to official Polish data, Poland, over the six years
of the war, lost approximately six million people, of whom
roughly three million were murdered Jews. No more than 300,000
Poles were killed in action. If one adds 700,000 to account for
refugees and natural wastage, that leaves two million of whom
certainly more than half are accounted for by the systematic
extermination measures against the leading classes. The re-
mainder can probably be ascribed to reprisals in the war against
the partisans, to the mass population transfers which were executed with extreme ruthlessness, and to the general intimidation
and terrorization by the occupation authorities.

4. German policy with regard to the Russian population in the
vast Russian territories occupied throughout two or three years
was entirely in line with the Polish policy just described: extermination of leading strata, deprivation of rights and enslavement
of the remaining mass of the population. Poland had originally
been earmarked by Hitler for a milder fate, that of an auxiliary
nation, like Hungary, Rumania, Slovakia and Bulgaria. When it
refused to play that part it was turned, not only as a punishment
for refusal but also as a preliminary exercise for Russia, into a trial
ground for the extermination and enslavement policy that had
always been planned for Russia. In the case of Russia, however,
there were two differences which further exacerbated this policy.

Firstly, the Russian upper classes were – in reality or by assumption – communist, whereas those of Poland had predominantly been conservative and Catholic, and this meant the drop-
ping of whatever inhibitions were left about their systematic
extermination. Secondly, in contrast to their attitude to Poland
the Wehrmacht was a willing participant in the crimes committed
in Russia.

In Poland, Colonel-General Blaskowitz, the first Military Commander of the occupied territory, was relieved of his post when he
expressed his horror during the first winter of the war in a
memorandum of complaints about the fact that behind the
German lines 'bestial and pathological instincts are raging unchecked'. Heydrich in his above-quoted report of 2 July 1940

pointed out that the 'extraordinarily radical' order by the Führer had not, of course, been communicated to all army commands, 'with the result that the action of the police and the ss assumed the outward appearance of brutal arbitrariness'. In Russia Hitler believed that he could no longer afford to let his army enjoy such innocence. As early as 30 March 1941, that is several months before the beginning of the war against Russia, he gave an address to senior officers in which he told them the unvarnished truth: 'We must move away from the point of view of soldierly comradeship. The communist is no comrade of ours either before or afterwards. This is a war of annihilation ... We are not waging war to preserve the enemy ... In the East hardness is mildness for the future.'

The extent to which the Wehrmacht Generals obeyed such injunctions, more particularly the extent to which Hitler's notorious order for the killing of all captured political commissars was obeyed, is a controversial point to this day. What is not controversial is the fate of Russian prisoners in German hands. According to a survey of the Wehrmacht General Office in the High Command of the Armed Forces of 1 May 1944, 5.16 million Russians had been taken prisoner up to that date, most of them in the first campaign of 1941. Of these 1,871,000 were still alive at that date; 473,000 were listed as 'executed', and 67,000 as escaped. The rest – nearly three million – had died in the POW cages, mostly starved to death. It is perfectly true that many German prisoners of war subsequently did not survive Russian captivity.

Here the borderline is blurred between the war crimes which are better forgotten and Hitler's mass murders. Certainly there were difficulties about feeding millions of prisoners taken within a few months, difficulties which can explain a lot, but they do not explain everything. That the starvation of prisoners and the emergence of cannibalism in the POW cages had been intended by Hitler is confirmed by his direct admission in an unexpected context. In his mid-day conference of 12 December 1942 Hitler justified his refusal to authorize a breakout of the Sixth Army from its encirclement at Stalingrad by, among other things, the argument that the horse artillery would then have to stay behind because the emaciated horses were no longer strong enough for haulage. Then he continued: 'If these were Russians I would say: One Russian eats another. But I cannot make one horse eat another.'

The mass murder of Russian civilians belonging to the leading strata was not the task of the Wehrmacht but that of four Special Operations Units which had been conducting the murder business behind the lines at high pressure from the first day onwards. By April 1942 – that is, over the first ten months of a four-year war – Special Operations Unit A (North) reported 250,000 'executed'; Special Operations Unit B (Centre) 70,000; Special Operations Unit C (South) 150,000; and Special Operations Unit D (extreme Southern Front) 90,000. As later figures have not reached us and as the reports do not differentiate between Jews and 'Bolsheviks', it is difficult to estimate the precise total of murdered non-Jewish Russian civilians. But it is certainly not likely to be lower than that in Poland – if anything, higher. We have already observed that by this mass murder Hitler, far from improving his chances of victory, on the contrary wrecked them.

5. Hitler's most extensive mass murder, as is well known, was committed against the Jews. At first, after mid-1941, this was against the Jews of Poland and Russia, and then, after the beginning of 1942, also against the Jews of Germany and the whole of occupied Europe which was, for this purpose, 'combed through from West to East'. The wished-for aim announced by Hitler in advance on 30 January 1939 was 'the annihilation of the Jewish race in Europe'. This final aim was not achieved, in spite of extreme efforts. Even so, the total of Jews murdered at Hitler's command amounts, according to the lowest calculations, to more than four million and according to the highest to nearly six million. Until 1942 the murders were carried out by mass shooting before mass graves which the victims had previously been forced to dig; subsequently in the six extermination camps of Treblinka, Sobibor, Maidanek (Lublin), Belzec, Chelmno (Kulmhof) and

Auschwitz, by gassing in specially constructed gas chambers to which huge crematoria were attached.

Recently an English historian, David Irving, has disputed Hitler's responsibility for the murder of the Jews, which, Irving claims, was performed by Himmler on his own initiative behind Hitler's back. Irving's thesis is untenable not only because it lacks all internal probability – under the conditions of the Third Reich it was totally impossible for an operation on that scale to be carried out without the knowledge, let alone against the wishes, of Hitler, not to mention the fact that Hitler himself had proclaimed in advance the 'annihilation of the Jewish race' in the event of war – but also because clear testimony, both of Hitler and of Himmler, proves that Hitler had given the orders and Himmler had executed them. Hitler publicly boasted of the implementation of his forecast on no fewer than five occasions in the course of 1942 (the first year of the 'Final Solution'): on 1 January, on 30 January, on 24 February, on 30 September and on 8 November. We shall quote the last statement verbatim:

You may still remember the meeting of the Reichstag when I declared: In case Jewry imagines that it can trigger off an international world war for the extermination of the European races, then the outcome will be not the extermination of the European races but the extermination of Jewry in Europe. I have always been laughed at as a prophet. Of those who then laughed a countless number are no longer laughing today, and those who are still laughing will perhaps no longer be doing so in a little while.

Himmler, too, repeatedly referred to his part in the attempted extermination of the Jews. But he did so in a totally different tone, not of bragging sneers but of self-pity. Thus on 5 May 1944: 'You will appreciate how hard it was for me to implement that military order given me, an order which I have followed and carried out from a sense of obedience and deepest conviction.' Or on 21 June 1944: 'It was the most terrible task and the most terrible instruction that could have been given to an organization: the instruction to solve the Jewish problem.' But no one other than Hitler was able to issue an 'instruction' or a 'military order'. There is scarcely any need for the additional testimony of Goebbels who, on 27 March 1942, refers in his diary to 'a procedure which is not too conspicuous' (the reference is to the first gas chambers which were being installed at Lublin at the beginning of 1942): 'A rather barbaric method, and one that need not be described more closely, is being applied here, and nothing much is left of the Jews themselves ... In this matter, too, the Führer is the unswerving protagonist and spokesman of a radical solution.'

Irving's only evidence in support of his thesis is a note made by Himmler on 30 November 1941, after a headquarter's conversation with Hitler: 'Jewish transport from Berlin, no liquidation.' In this one instance Hitler evidently ordered an exception to be made, which in itself proves that 'liquidation' was the rule and, moreover, that Hitler concerned himself even with the details of this murder operation. It is also easy to see why the exception was made; the Jewish transport from Berlin had been premature; it was not yet the turn of the German Jews. In November 1941 the 'liquidation' of the Polish and Russian Jews was still in full swing whereas the 'Final Solution' for the whole of Europe was not organized until the Wannsee Conference of 20 January 1942, and there had to be order in everything. Besides, the gas chambers and cremating furnaces were not yet ready. They only went into operation, one at a time, in 1942.

Nevertheless the episode picked out by Irving casts an interesting light on two aspects which deserve closer examination. One of these concerns the handling of the mass murder of the Jews among the German public and the other concerns Hitler's timetable for this, his numerically greatest, crime.

Hitler, as we have just shown, publicly boasted of that crime on no less than five occasions in the course of 1942, but only in general terms. As for the details, he had those kept secret within Germany as far as possible, evidently because he did not expect approbation but on the contrary an unwelcome disquiet, and perhaps even instances of opposition of the kind that had impeded the 'Mercy Death Programme'.

Prior to the war Hitler had twice tested the reaction of the German population to open violence against the Jews – once during the nationwide boycott of Jewish businesses by the SA on 1 April 1933 and again during the equally nationwide large-scale pogrom (also ordered from above) of 9 and 10 November 1938 which to this day has come to be known as the 'Reichskristall-nacht', the night of shattered glass. The result, from his point of view, had been negative on both occasions. The German masses had not taken part; on the contrary, there had been numerous instances of pity for the Jews, anger and shame, although admit-tedly no more than that. There was never any open rebellion, and the term 'Reichskristallnacht' which, no one knows how, was immediately on everybody's lips, clearly reflected the embarrassed dilemma in which the average German found himself in the face of the misdeeds of November 1938 – on the one hand derision and rejection, and on the other an anxious wish not to perceive the real horror of what had happened and instead to play the whole thing down to smashed window panes.

Hitler acted in line with these findings as far as Germany was concerned. He did not spare the German Jews anything, but he was careful to provide the mass of Germans with the opportunity of remaining in ignorance or of deluding themselves that things were not as bad as all that. The extermination operations were taking place far outside Germany, deep in Eastern Europe, where Hitler could count on more local approbation and where, more-over, murder had been the order of the day since the outbreak of the war. For the Germans, officially, the Jews were merely being 'resettled'; Hitler even, whenever possible, went so far as not to have the German Jews transported direct to the extermination camps but first had them taken to the huge ghetto of Theresien-stadt in Bohemia, whence they were able for a while to send post-cards to their German friends – before being moved on to Auschwitz.

Of course, a lot of what was happening there seeped through

into Germany in spite of everything. But anyone positively wishing to remain in ignorance could do so, or could at least feign
ignorance, even to himself. And that was what most Germans did,
as incidentally did most of the citizens of the other European
countries from which the Jews were being 'combed out'. Any
action against it would have put them all in danger of their lives,
and besides they had a war to worry about and plenty of anxieties
of their own. The most an individual could risk was emergency
aid to enable personal Jewish friends to submerge, and that happened even in Germany, though not as frequently as, for instance,
in Holland or Denmark. To prevent the crime altogether would
have required a revolt – and how was that to be accomplished
under conditions of war and dictatorship? At least Hitler's mass
murders played some honour-saving part as a motivation for the
conspirators of 20 July. Count Schwerin-Schwanenfeld, ques-
tioned about his motives by the People's Court in the trial of the
conspirators, had just about time to say: 'I thought of the many
murders – ' before Freisler, the president of the People's Tribunal,
shouted him down.

The charge of having allowed these things to happen, which
will stick to the Germans for a long time yet, is not our subject
here. We are concerned with Hitler. And it certainly is interesting
to notice that where his greatest crime was concerned he did not
take his fellow countrymen fully into his confidence because he
did not trust them. In spite of all the anti-semitic propaganda
during the preceding ten years he did not expect them to be ready
for the mass murder of their Jewish fellow citizens. He had not
been able to turn them into that 'Master Race' that would flinch
from nothing, the ideal he had dreamed of. And this may well be
one of the reasons why, during the final years, he increasingly
despised them, why he no longer sought contact with them, why
he became increasingly indifferent to their fate, and why eventually he even turned his destructive intentions against them. That
will be discussed in the next and final chapter.

But let us once more return to Irving's sole evidence exonerating
Hitler – his instruction to Himmler of 30 November 1941 for the

Jewish transport which had left Berlin that day not to be liquidated. The date is interesting. It is five days before the Russian
counter-offensive at Moscow, which convinced Hitler that the war
could no longer be won; ten days before his declaration of war on
America, with which he sealed his defeat; and fifty days before the
Wannsee Conference at which the 'Final Solution of the Jewish
problem' was organized, that is, the murder of the Jews in
Germany, as well as the rest of Europe, in death factories. Until
then the systematic murder of the Jews had been confined to
Poland and Russia, and its cumbersome method had been mass
shooting.

There is a clear connection between the three dates. So long as
Hitler was still hoping to achieve in Russia a similarly rapid
victory as a year before in France, he was also hoping that Britain
would come to terms since in Russia she would have lost her last
'continental sword'. He had often said so. But in that case he must
not appear as a mass murderer in countries where anything that
happened became instantly known in Britain. What he was doing
in Poland and in Russia could, so he had reason to hope, be kept
secret from the outside world at least while the war was on, but
mass murder in France, Holland, Belgium, Luxembourg, Denmark, Norway, and even Germany itself, would become immediately known in Britain and would make Hitler totally
unacceptable there – which is what actually happened. The pro-
clamation of 'punishment for these crimes' as a new Western war
aim dates from January 1942.

In other words, Hitler would only be able to fulfil his long-
cherished wish to exterminate the Jews from the whole of Europe
if he abandoned all hope of a negotiated peace with Britain (and
the associated hope of preventing America from joining the war).
And that he only did after 5 December 1941, the day when the
Russian offensive at Moscow rudely awakened him from his
dreams of victory in Russia. This must have come as an extraordinary shock to him; only two months previously he had
publicly announced 'that this opponent is already on the ground
and will never rise again'. And under the impact of that shock he

now changed course, 'icily cold' and 'quick as lightning'. If he could no longer be victorious in Russia then, so Hitler argued, there was also no chance left of peace with Britain. He might therefore also declare war on America straight away, a step which, after Roosevelt's long unanswered provocations, gave him patent satisfaction. And he could also indulge in the even greater satisfaction of giving orders now for the 'Final Solution of the Jewish problem' for the whole of Europe, since he no longer needed to consider the effect that this crime would have in Britain or America. At the same time he also made Germany's defeat inevitable and moreover ensured that defeat would be followed by judgement. But he had already observed that this would not bother him when on 27 November in his conversation (mentioned in the preceding chapter) with the Danish and Croat Foreign Ministers he had expressed himself to the effect that if Germany could not be victorious then it might as well perish, he would not shed any tears over it.

In short, in December 1941, within a few days, Hitler made his final choice between the two incompatible aims which he had pursued from the outset – German domination of the world and the extermination of the Jews. He abandoned the former as unattainable and entirely concentrated on the latter. (On 30 November it had still been a few days too early for that.) Moreover, he now even accepted Germany's total defeat with all the possible consequences as the price of being able to carry out at last the extermination of the Jews throughout Europe, a plan which had long made his mouth water.

This also now explains his declaration of war on America, a step we were unable, in the preceding chapter, to explain from any political point of view. In December 1941 Hitler the politician finally abdicated in favour of Hitler the mass murderer.

We now also have an explanation of Hitler's complete inactivity and lethargy during the second half of the war, an attitude we had occasion to wonder about in the preceding chapter and which so strikingly contrasted with his earlier political alertness and resolution. Politics, for which he had so much talent, no longer interested Hitler; he had no need of it for the sole objective he was now pursuing. 'Politics? I no longer make politics. It disgusts me so.' This remark (to Ribbentrop's liaison man at the Führer's headquarters, Hewel) was admittedly made at a later date, in the spring of 1945, but it could equally well have been made at any time since 1942. From the end of 1941 onwards Hitler no longer made German politics. He only engaged in murderous extravaganzas.

What Hitler continued to concern himself with, and more intensively than ever, was the military conduct of the war. This he still needed in order to gain the time in which to carry out his intended mass murder and to hold the territory in which he found his victims. His strategy in the years after 1942 was exclusively aimed at gaining time and holding territory. Initiatives for spectacular isolated military successes, such as might have given a man other than Hitler a chance of a negotiated peace, Hitler no longer developed after the beginning of 1943. Whenever individual generals took such initiatives (Rommel in Africa in the summer of 1942, Manstein in the Ukraine in the spring of 1943) he no longer supported them. If anything, he obstructed them. They no longer interested him.

All the evidence is that since the turn of the year 1941/42 he had inwardly come to terms with eventual defeat. Indeed his still famous statement, rather revealing in its ambiguity, 'As a matter of principle I never stop until five minutes past twelve', dates from November 1942. The fact that, throughout these years, while the ring around Germany was closing ever more tightly, he continued in his table talk at headquarters to reveal an often unimpaired self-satisfaction and at times even robust merriment, can only be explained by his knowledge that his now sole objective was moving closer towards realization every day, just as the Allied armies were drawing closer to a gutted and bombed Germany. For three years, day after day, Jewish families throughout Europe were taken from their homes or hiding places, transported to the East and driven naked into the death factories, where the chimneys of the cremating furnaces smoked day and night. During those three years

Hitler no longer enjoyed successes, as during the preceding eleven years. However, he found it easy to do without them since, more than ever before, he was now able to indulge the delights of the killer who has shed his last restraints, has his victims in his grip and deals with them as he wishes.

To Hitler, during the last three and a half years of war, the war had become a kind of race which he was still hoping to win. Who would reach his goal sooner, Hitler with his extermination of the Jews or the Allies with their military overthrow of Germany? It took the Allies three and a half years to reach their goal. And in the meantime Hitler, too, had certainly come terrifyingly close to his.

Betrayal

I T is an interesting but, strangely enough, scarcely noted fact that Hitler by no means did the greatest harm to those nations against whom he committed his greatest crimes.

The Soviet Union, as a result of Hitler, lost at least twelve million lives – according to her own claims twenty million – but the tremendous efforts which Hitler compelled her to make raised her to the position of a superpower which she did not hold before. In Poland Hitler killed six million people – or, if one does not include the Polish Jews, three million – but the outcome of Hitler's war is a geographically sounder and nationally more homogeneous Poland than pre-war Poland had been. Hitler had intended to exterminate the Jews – within his sphere of power he almost succeeded – but his attempt, which cost the lives of between four and six million of them, gave the survivors that energy of desperation that was needed for the creation of a Jewish state. For the first time in nearly 2,000 years the Jews, because of Hitler, have once more a state – a proud and glorious state. Without Hitler there would have been no Israel.

Hitler inflicted far greater objective damage on Britain against whom he did not even want to wage war and always conducted war half-heartedly and with half his strength. Britain, as a result of Hitler's war, has lost its empire and is no longer the world power it used to be; a similar diminution of stature has been suffered, owing to Hitler, by France and most other countries and nations of Western Europe.

But Hitler inflicted by far the greatest damage, in any objective view, on Germany. The Germans, too, made a terrible sacrifice to Hitler – over seven million souls. They lost more than the Jews and the Poles; only the Russians suffered an even greater blood-letting. The casualty lists of the remaining participants of the war do not compare with these four. But whereas the Soviet Union and Poland, following their terrible blood-letting, are today stronger than before, and whereas Israel owes its very existence to the

149

Jewish blood sacrifice, the German Reich has disappeared from the map.

Thanks to Hitler, Germany not only suffered the same diminution of status as all the other former great powers of Western Europe, it lost one-quarter of its former national territory (its 'living space') and what was left was divided. The two states resulting from that division have, by integration into antagonistic power blocs, been forced into an unnaturally hostile relationship. The fact that one can again live well today, at least in the bigger one of the two, the Federal Republic, owes nothing to Hitler. In 1945 Hitler left Germany a desert – a physical desert and, what is all too readily forgotten, also a political desert. He left not only the corpses, the rubble, the ruins and millions of starving, drifting people, but also a collapsed administration and a wrecked state. Both – the misery of the people and the destruction of the state – he deliberately brought about during the final months of the war. He had intended even worse: his final programme for Germany was national death. In his final phase, if not before, Hitler became a deliberate traitor to Germany.

This is no longer realized to quite the same extent by the younger generation of Germans living today as it is by those who witnessed it. The Hitler of the last few months of his life has become a legend – not a flattering legend but nevertheless one which, in a sense, clears him of responsibility for the agony of Germany in 1945. According to that legend Hitler was only a shadow of himself during the final phase of the war, an exceedingly sick man, a human wreck, stripped of his resolution and watching the disaster around him as though paralysed. He had, according to the picture that emerges from the popular accounts of the months from January to April 1945, lost all control over events and from his bunker he was directing armies which no longer existed. He alternated between uncontrollable fits of fury and lethargic resignation, and to the very last moment he babbled of final victory among the ruins of Berlin. In short, he had become blind to reality and, in a sense, of unsound mind.

This picture omits the main thing. Of course Hitler's state of health in 1945 was no longer of the best; of course he had aged and five years of war had left their mark on his nerves (as indeed they had on Churchill's and Roosevelt's); and certainly he frightened his entourage by his increasingly frequent black moods and explosions of fury. But in the temptation to paint all this in effective black and sulphurous hues and indulge in a twilight-of-the-gods atmosphere one fact is often overlooked – that during those final months Hitler once more reached the peak of his performance where resolution and determination were concerned. A certain paralysis of will, a rigidity, an unimaginative routine was present during the preceding period, in 1943, when Goebbels in his diaries worriedly noted a 'Führer crisis', and during the first six months of 1944. But face to face with defeat Hitler was again all there, as if galvanized. His hand might shake, but the grip of that shaking hand was still, or again, sudden and deadly. The teeth-gnashing resolve and hectic activity of a physically declining Hitler during the months from August 1944 to April 1945 was astonishing. It might, in a certain sense, even be called admirable, except that it was ever more clearly, and in the end unambiguously, directed towards an unsuspected goal – the total ruin of Germany. This to many people nowadays may seem implausible.

At the beginning this was not yet clearly discernible, but at the end it was unmistakable. Hitler's policy during that final phase had three clearly distinguishable phases. During the first (August to October 1944) he successfully prevented the discontinuation of the lost war and made sure there would be a fight to the finish. During the second (November 1944 to January 1945) he made a surprising last sortie – to the West. But during the third (February to April 1945), with the same energy he had devoted to his conquests until 1941 and from 1942 to 1944 to the annihilation of the Jews, he pursued the total destruction of Germany. In order to see how this final goal of Hitler's was gradually taking shape we must take a closer look at Hitler's activities during the last nine months of the war.

The military situation at the end of August 1944 was a fairly accurate replica of that of September 1918, when the then

German military dictator, Ludendorff, had thrown in the sponge. In 1918, as in 1944, defeat, as far as was humanly predictable, could no longer be averted, and the end was in sight, although no enemy soldier had yet stepped upon German soil. In 1918 it would probably have been as possible to drag out the war until the following year, as it was done in 1944/45.

In that situation, as is well known, Ludendorff had come to the conclusion that, in his own words, 'the war must be brought to an end'. He had insisted that an armistice be asked for, and he had invited his political opponents into the government in order to make the request for an armistice more credible and to give Germany representatives who were less discredited and more capable of negotiations. By subsequently accusing the receivers in bankruptcy whom he himself had appointed ('let them face the music') of having stabbed the undefeated Army in the back he later put his action of September 1918 in an ugly light. But viewed in itself his action at the time was that of a responsible patriot who, faced with imminent defeat, determined to spare his country the worst and to save what could be saved.

Hitler on 22 August 1944 did the exact opposite of what Ludendorff had done on 29 September 1918. In an 'Operation Thunderstorm' he at one blow ordered the arrest and detention of some 5,000 former Ministers, mayors, Members of Parliament, party leaders and political civil servants of the Weimar Republic, including, incidentally, Konrad Adenauer and Kurt Schumacher, the two subsequent protagonists during the founding period of the Federal Republic. This was precisely the group of people whom Ludendorff, in an analogous situation, had entrusted with the government and the liquidation of the war – in a sense Germany's political reserve. Ludendorff had placed them at the helm in the face of defeat; Hitler, in the same situation, eliminated them. The operation, unpublicized at the time, has remained strangely unnoticed even by historians; and it is usually linked with the persecution of the conspirators of 20 July with which it had nothing to do. Instead, it was the first indication that Hitler wanted to prevent any possible repetition of what in his opinion had been the premature suspension of the war in 1918, an indication that he was determined, even without perceptible hope, to fight on to the bitter end. He had put it as 'until five minutes past twelve' – and he would not let anyone stop him.

With regard to this action it is still possible to hold different views on his decision. Throughout history there have always been in the event of defeat two schools of thought and two paths of action which one might call the practical and the heroic. The one aims at saving as much of the substance as possible, the other at leaving behind an inspiring legend. There is something to be said for each of them. It might be said for the latter that the future is never entirely predictable and that what may seem inescapable might sometimes still be averted. German history has the famous example of Frederick the Great who in 1762 found himself in the same situation as Ludendorff in 1918 and Hitler in 1944 and who, nevertheless, by the 'miracle of the House of Brandenburg' – Russia's unforeseen change of sovereign and alliance – had been saved. Had he given up, that saving accident would have come too late. True, miracles are the exception in history, not the rule, and anyone counting on them is playing a lottery with few winning tickets.

The example of Frederick was rather overworked by German propaganda during the final year of the war, but it is doubtful whether it really played a major part in Hitler's motives. Surely a modern national war is something different from the cabinet wars of the eighteenth century. It is far more plausible to assign the decisive role among Hitler's motives to the negative example of November 1918. Let us recall that November 1918 had been Hitler's arousing experience. His tears of fury at a war, in his view, given up prematurely as lost were an unforgettable early experience. His determination never again to allow a November 1918 to happen was the main original impulse that drove him to become a politician. Now, in a sense, Hitler had reached his original goal: another November 1918 was just around the corner, and Hitler this time was in a position to prevent it. He was determined to do just that.

Nor should one entirely lose sight of his hatred of the German 'November criminals', a hatred overwhelming in 1918 and now once more flaring up – a hatred of his fellow countrymen. In *Mein Kampf* Hitler had quoted, with grim endorsement, the alleged dictum of a British journalist in 1918: 'Every third German is a traitor.' Now he ordered any German who uttered the obvious and current thought that the war was lost and who hinted that he wished to survive it to be mercilessly hanged or beheaded. Hitler had always been a great hater and derived much inward pleasure from killing. The force of Hitler's hatred, the homicidal drive in Hitler which had raged for years against Jews, Poles and Russians, was now quite openly turning against Germans.

Be that as it may, in the late summer and early autumn of 1944 Hitler once more displayed an energy and vigour that was reminiscent of his strongest periods. By the end of August there had scarcely been a front line any longer in the West; even in the East it had been, in Hitler's own words, 'more holes than front line'. By the end of October both fronts were once more holding, the Allied offensive had been halted, and at home Hitler had mobilized the *Volkssturm*. All men from sixteen to sixty had been mobilized for a people's war. As for fighting morale, Hitler kept it up by zealously disseminated propaganda rumours about a miracle weapon he still had up his sleeve. In reality, of course, it was not Germany that had the atom bomb, the real miracle weapon of 1945, but America. It is a strange thought that the prolonged, bitter and costly total defensive war which Hitler desired and for which he got Germany into trim in the autumn of 1944, if it had materialized would have drawn the first atom bombs upon Germany instead of upon Japan.

But Hitler himself saw to it that it did not come to this because he immediately squandered the forces he had scraped together for that defensive war. In November 1944 he decided once more to take the offensive – in the West. On 16 December 1944 the Germans launched their last attack in the Ardennes.

In contrast to all the other military episodes of the Second World War we have to take a closer look now at the Ardennes offensive, because this was more than an episode. To it Germany owed the zonal boundaries of occupation which eventually became dividing frontiers. And with it began Hitler's turning against his own country.

The Ardennes offensive was, more than any other operation of the Second World War, Hitler's very own work. It was, from a military point of view, an insane enterprise. At the time a military offensive, in order to be successful, required a superiority of at least three to one. The ratio of forces on the Western Front, however, in December 1944 was, for the German side on land, less than one to one, not to mention the overwhelming Allied superiority in the air. The weaker was 'having a go' at the stronger. In order to achieve at least a bare momentary superiority on the localized sector of the offensive, Hitler had moreover been obliged to strip his defensive front in the East right down to the bones, and he had done so in spite of the desperate warnings of his then Chief of General Staff Guderian that the Russians were massing for a huge offensive. Hitler, therefore, took a double gamble. If the offensive in the West failed, which was to be expected considering the ratio of forces, then it would use up forces needed for a subsequent defence of the western territory of the Reich. At the same time that offensive was making any defence in the East hopeless if the Russians attacked – which was likewise to be expected.

Both things, in fact, happened. The Ardennes offensive failed and the Russians attacked. Though initially favoured by foggy weather which kept the Allied air forces grounded, the offensive only scored slight successes in the week before Christmas. Then the skies cleared, and over Christmas the two German tank armies which had launched the attack were smashed from the air. During the first week of January their battered remnants were rolled back to their starting positions, and on 12 January the Russians overran the thin screen which was all that was left of the German Eastern Front. In one swoop they moved forward from the Vistula to the Oder. All this had been predicted, and indeed Guderian had repeatedly rehearsed it to Hitler with desperate insistence. But

Hitler did not want to listen. The Ardennes offensive had been his own personal idea – his last but one idea (we shall come to know the last one presently); and he insisted on its execution with all his obduracy.

Why did he insist? The answer is a riddle to this day. Military reasons can be ruled out. Hitler was not the green amateur in military matters that he is nowadays often depicted as. With his military knowledge he could have had no illusions about his operation's prospect of success. That he conjured up illusions of success to the officers involved (whom he had previously assembled in order to encourage them) does not prove that he shared those illusions.

A more likely guess would be foreign policy motives. An offensive in the West, even if it proved unsuccessful, might be a signal to the Western statesmen that Hitler now regarded them and no longer Russia as the chief enemy, that he would employ his entire remaining strength in the West, even if as a result the whole of Germany were to become Russian-occupied territory. One can conjecture that Hitler wanted to face the Western Powers with the alternative of either a National Socialist or a Bolshevized Germany, that he wanted to confront them with the question 'Whom would you rather see on the Rhine – Stalin or me?' And it is possible that he still believed they would prefer him. In which, of course, he was wrong – *if* he believed it. Roosevelt was convinced in 1945 that he could work together profitably with Stalin. Churchill did not share that conviction, but faced with a choice he, too, would have preferred Stalin to Hitler. Hitler had made himself totally unacceptable in the West by his mass murders, but it is conceivable that he did not understand it, any more than Himmler who, after all, approached the Western Powers as late as April with the naïve offer of a surrender in the West followed by a common continuation of the war in the East. Even *if* he saw it there are indications that, faced with a choice himself, he really preferred defeat in the East in 1945 to defeat in the West. His German fellow countrymen viewed the approaching Russian wave with horror, so much so that many of them about that time were beginning to look forward to American or British occupation as though to salvation. Hitler's respect for Stalin had grown in the course of the war, whereas for Churchill and Roosevelt he had developed a profound hatred. One may visualize a double-bottomed argument on Hitler's part roughly on the following lines. Perhaps his unexpected demonstration of supreme militant resolution in the West combined with acceptance of the threatening defeat in the East will after all give the Western Powers a fright that might, even at this last moment, make them ready for compromise. If it did not – never mind. There really will be a defeat in the East and let the Western Powers see what they make of that. It is, admittedly, a contorted line of argument.

Hitler's thinking, however, appears far less complicated if one assumes that his principal motive by then was no longer governed by foreign but by domestic policy, and was in fact directed against his own nation. Between the mass of the German population and Hitler a gulf had opened in the autumn of 1944. The mass of the Germans no longer wanted the hopeless fight to the finish that Hitler wanted. They wanted an end, just as in the autumn of 1918; and they wanted as lenient an end as was possible, which was in the West. To keep the Russians out and let the Western Powers in had become the last secret war aim of most Germans by the end of 1944. And that Hitler was still able to spoil for them by his Ardennes offensive. He could not have everybody beheaded who thought such thoughts because there were too many of them and most of them were careful not to speak their thoughts out loud. But he was able to make sure that if they did not follow him through hell and high water they would be left at the mercy of Russian vengeance. They would be sorry for hoping for a liberating occupation by GIs and Tommies – that he was grimly determined to make sure. Seen in that light, the Ardennes offensive, which from a military point of view was pure insanity and from a foreign policy one at best a wild speculation, suddenly makes sense; and that is why it is probably correct to see it in that light. But it also means that by then Hitler was pursuing a policy against Germany and against the Germans.

This view is supported also by the fact that, with his Ardennes offensive, Hitler clearly abandoned his defensive concept of August 1944. That concept had aimed at terror without end. There was to be rigid delaying resistance on all fronts and where the armies had to give ground a total people's war in all lost regions. The Ardennes offensive, on the other hand, was aimed instead towards an end with terror, a burning up of his last military forces in one last hopeless offensive battle. If one asks oneself why Hitler suddenly changed his mind then the answer stares one in the face. He saw that his total people's war would not materialize, because the mass of the German people did not want it. That mass no longer thought or felt the way Hitler thought or felt. Very well, they were to be punished for it – punished by death. That was Hitler's last decision.

One may argue whether this was already reflected, though unspoken, in the Ardennes offensive, but it certainly acquired clear and irrefutable shape in the Führer orders of 18 and 19 March 1945 by which Hitler condemned Germany to national death.

At that time the Russians were on the Oder and the Americans had crossed the Rhine. There was no longer any question of holding them; the meeting between Western and Eastern Allies in the middle of Germany was only a matter of weeks. The reaction of the population, however, differed very markedly between the eastern and western zones of operation and retreat. In the East the people were fleeing in vast numbers; in the West they stayed put, hung out tablecloths and bed linen from their windows in token of surrender and frequently implored the German officers no longer to defend their village or town and instead to save them from destruction at the last hour.

To this attitude of the population in the West of his country Hitler gave his answer in the first of the two Führer orders, the one of 18 March. He commanded that the western German invasion areas were 'to be cleared immediately of all inhabitants, starting behind the main zone of military operations'. The order was drafted at the Military Staff Conference that day and, untypically, there was opposition to it. Albert Speer, Hitler's former architect and at that time Minister of Armaments, today the last surviving witness of Hitler's final phase, reports on it as follows:

One of the generals present tried to persuade Hitler that it was impossible to carry out the evacuation of hundreds of thousands. Surely there were no more trains available. Transport had long since totally broken down. Hitler remained unmoved. 'Then let them march on foot!' he replied. That, too, could not be organized, the general objected; that would require food supplies, the human stream would have to be guided through thinly populated areas and, besides, the people lacked the necessary footwear. He was not allowed to finish. Unimpressed, Hitler turned his back on him.

That first order to despatch all of the inhabitants of the German West, without food supplies, on a march that had no destination and that might be called a death march, was already tantamount to mass murder, this time committed against Germans. The second Führer order of 19 March, the so-called 'Nero order', revealed with complete clarity his intention of depriving the Germans, and this time *all* Germans, of any hope of survival. Its decisive paragraph reads:

All military, transport, communication, industrial and supply facilities, as well as material assets within the Reich territory which the enemy might in any way whatever make use of for the continuation of his struggle, either now or in the foreseeable future, are to be destroyed.

And when Speer protested, Hitler, according to Speer's testimony, added the following explanation 'in an icy voice':

If the war is lost then the nation will be lost also. There is no need to show any consideration for the foundations which the German nation needs for its most primitive survival. On the contrary, it is better to destroy those things ourselves. Because this nation has shown itself the weaker, and the future belongs exclusively to the stronger nation from the East. In any event, what remains after this struggle are only the inferior, for the good have died in battle.

One is reminded of the remark made by Hitler as long ago as 27 November 1941, when the possibility of failure had first emerged, an observation we have already quoted. Let us recall it. Hitler then had said: 'On this point, too, I am icily cold. If one day the German nation is no longer sufficiently strong or sufficiently ready for sacrifice to stake its blood for its existence, then let it perish and be annihilated by some other stronger power ... I shall shed no tears for the German nation.' Now the time had come and he was serious about it.

Hitler's two orders of 18 and 19 March 1945 were not fully carried out. If they had been, then, as Goebbels remarked about the Jews three years before, nothing much would have been left of the Germans. Speer did his best to sabotage the implementation of the destruction order. There were also other Party officials who shrank from these ultimate steps; and frequently indeed those directly affected offered resistance, with more or less success, to the destruction of their basis of livelihood. Eventually the rapid advance of the Allies, by then rarely delayed by serious resistance, saw to it that the Germans were saved the full severity of the fate that Hitler had ultimately assigned to them.

One must not imagine that Hitler's last orders were just spoken to the winds and no longer produced any consequences. In mid-March 1945 considerable parts of Germany were not yet occupied. In them a Führer order was still the supreme law and there were still fanatics among Party and ss officials who thought and felt like their Führer. For the next six weeks they were vying with the enemy air forces and the enemy artillery in the final destruction of Germany, and there are many reports suggesting that during the final weeks of the war the German population of many

German towns and rural areas found themselves between two fires and came to fear their own demolition squads and ss patrols more than the enemy.

And in fact Hitler's resolution, which they were now implementing, was more brutal than the enemy's. The enemy armies, certainly the Western armies, were not out to destroy 'the foundations which the German nation needs for its most primitive survival'. The result, therefore, was that the enemy occupation, which was now rapidly proceeding, was overwhelmingly welcomed as a relief, at least in the West. The Americans, British and French, who had expected to find a nation of National Socialists, instead encountered a thoroughly disenchanted nation that no longer wished to have anything to do with Hitler. At that time the conquerors often regarded this as servile dissimulation but it was that only in the rarest of cases. The people really felt betrayed by their Führer, and justly so. The 're-education' which the Allies had intended to practise had been most drastically performed by Hitler himself during his last few weeks. During those weeks the Germans were like a woman whose lover suddenly reveals himself as her would-be murderer and who runs screaming to her neighbours for help.

Let us put the facts quite clearly: in his annihilation orders of 18 and 19 March 1945 Hitler was no longer concerned with a heroic fight to the finish, as he still had been in the autumn of 1944. A heroic fight to the finish could not be served by despatching hundreds of thousands on a death march to the interior of the country and simultaneously ordering the destruction there of everything they would need for their most primitive survival. The only purpose of that last mass murder action of Hitler's directed against Germany was to punish the Germans for not having been willing to embrace a heroic fight to the finish. In other words they were being punished for having refused the last role allotted to them by Hitler, in Hitler's eyes a crime deserving death – it had always been that. Hitler had always believed that a nation refusing to accept the role assigned to it must die, and in that respect his murderous actions against the Germans at the end of the war represents a strange parallel to his murderous actions against the Poles at its beginning.

Originally the Poles had by no means been scheduled for mass murder the way the Jews and the Russians had. The role assigned to them had instead been similar to that allotted to the Romanians: the role of a subordinate ally and auxiliary nation in the war of conquest against Russia Hitler had always planned. Their refusal to play this role had been the real reason for Hitler's war against Poland. It was certainly not Danzig which had for years with complete Polish agreement been governed by a National Socialist Senate entirely in line with Hitler's desires. Danzig was merely a pretext. The interesting point, however, is that, having won the war against Poland militarily, Hitler by no means used his victory for realizing his original objective, which was to force the Poles to enter the alliance they had previously refused. This would have been politically consistent and in the prevailing situation would probably not have been impossible. But instead he made Poland the object of a pointless, raging five-year orgy of punishment and revenge, giving full vent for the first time to his destructive instinct and switching off his political reason. The fact is that within Hitler, alongside the highly gifted politician there had always lurked a mass murderer. And though his lust for murder had originally seized only on Jews and Russians as victims, wherever his intentions were crossed that lust for murder overrode political reasoning. Thus it had been at the beginning of the war in Poland and thus it was at the end of the war in Germany.

Of course, Hitler had assigned to the Germans a far greater role than he had, at the time, to the Poles: first that of a world-conquering master race; then at least that of a world-resisting race of heroes. But even the Germans did not toe the line in the end, no matter whether from weakness or from punishable recalcitrance. And so they, too, ultimately came under Hitler's sentence of death: they were to 'perish and be annihilated', to quote him once more.

Hitler's relationship with Germany had shown some strange features from the start. A few English historians during the war tried to prove that Hitler was, as it were, the predetermined product of the whole of German history; that there was a straight line from Luther through Frederick the Great and Bismarck to Hitler. The opposite is true. Hitler does not stand in any German tradition, least of all the Protestant–Prussian tradition which, not excluding Frederick and Bismarck, had been a tradition of sober selfless service to the welfare of the state. But sober selfless service to the welfare of the state is the last thing that Hitler, even the successful Hitler of the pre-war years, can be credited with. The German state, not only constitutionally but administratively, had been sacrificed by him from the start to his idea of the total mobilization of the forces of the people and, lest it be forgotten, to his own indismissibility and irreplaceability. This has been shown in earlier chapters. He deliberately replaced soberness by mass intoxication; one might say that for six years he dispensed himself to the Germans like a drug which he then abruptly withdrew from them during the war. And as for unselfishness, Hitler surely was the extreme example of a politician who places his personal mission above all else and who makes politics by the yardstick of his personal biography. If we recall the presentation of his political ideology we are again struck by the fact that he did not think in terms of states at all but of nations and races. This, incidentally, explains the brutality of his political operations and, at the same time, his inability to translate military victories into political successes. The political civilization of Europe – including, of course, Germany – had, ever since the Migration of the Peoples, been based on keeping wars and the consequences of wars within the system of states and on leaving nations and races untouched.

Hitler was no statesman, and that alone puts him outside German history. But one cannot even properly call him a man of the people, as perhaps one might Luther. He shares with Luther only the fact of being unique in German history, without predecessors and without successors. Luther in many respects positively personifies the German national character; Hitler's personality fits into the German national character in roughly the way his Party Rally structures fitted into Nuremberg – in other words, sticking out like a sore thumb. The Germans, incidentally, preserved a certain awareness of just that even at the time of their most devout faith in the Führer. Their admiration always had in it a trace of astonishment at the fact that something so unexpected and so strange as Hitler had been vouchsafed them. Hitler to them was a miracle, a 'godsend', which, put more prosaically, means someone inexplicably blown in from outside. And 'from outside' in this case did not just mean from Austria. To the Germans, Hitler had always seemed to come from a long way off – first, for a while, from high heaven; later, may the Lord have mercy on us, from the deepest abysses of hell.

Did he love the Germans? He had chosen Germany without knowing Germany. Strictly speaking he never came to know it. The Germans were his chosen people because his inborn power instinct pointed to them like a compass needle as to the greatest power potential in Europe in his day – which in fact they were. And it was only as an instrument of power that he was ever genuinely interested in them. He had great ambitions for Germany, and in that he found himself at one with the Germans of his generation. The Germans of that time were an ambitious nation – ambitious and at the same time politically perplexed.

The combination offered Hitler his chance. But German ambition and Hitler's ambition for Germany were not identical – what German ever wanted to settle in Russia? – and Hitler lacked the ear for nuance. Once in power he certainly stopped listening. His ambition for Germany increasingly resembled the ambition a pedigree breeder and racing stud owner has for his horses. And in the end Hitler acted like a bad-tempered and disappointed stud owner who has his best horse whipped to death because it proved unable to win the Derby.

The annihilation of Germany was the last goal Hitler set himself. He was not able to attain it fully, any more than his other annihilation goals. What he did achieve was that Germany cut loose from him in the end – more quickly than expected and also more thoroughly. Thirty-three years after Napoleon's final over-throw a new Napoleon was elected in France to be President of the Republic. Thirty-three years after Hitler's suicide no one in Germany professing Hitler and wishing to take up his heritage has even the slightest political outsider's chance. This is surely all to the good. What is less good is that the memory of Hitler is being suppressed by the older Germans and that most of the younger generation no longer know the first thing about him. Still less good is that since Hitler many Germans no longer dare to be patriots. For German history does not end with Hitler. Anyone believing that it does, and possibly even rejoicing at it, does not realize just how much he is thereby fulfilling Hitler's last will and testament.